Jane Austen for Kids

Her Life, Writings, and World

WITH 21 ACTIVITIES

NANCY I. SANDERS

CHICAGO
REVIEW
PRESS

Copyright © 2019 by Nancy I. Sanders
All rights reserved
Published by Chicago Review Press Incorporated
814 North Franklin Street
Chicago, Illinois 60610
ISBN 978-1-61373-853-5

Library of Congress Cataloging-in-Publication Data
Names: Sanders, Nancy I. author.
Title: Jane Austen for kids : her life, writings, and world
  with 21 activities / Nancy I. Sanders.
Description: Chicago : Chicago Review Press, 2018. |
Includes bibliographical
  references and index.
Identifiers: LCCN 2018009544 (print) | LCCN 2018012585
(ebook) | ISBN
  9781613738542 (adobe pdf) | ISBN 9781613738559 (epub)
| ISBN 9781613738566
  (kindle) | ISBN 9781613738535 (trade paper)
Subjects: LCSH: Austen, Jane, 1775–1817—Juvenile litera-
ture. | Novelists,
  English—19th century—Biography—Juvenile literature.
| Austen, Jane,
  1775-1817—Study and teaching (Elementary) —Activity
programs. | Austen,
  Jane, 1775-1817--Study and teaching (Middle school) —
Activity programs.
Classification: LCC PR4036 (ebook) | LCC PR4036 .S225
2018 (print) | DDC
  823/.7 [B] —dc23
LC record available at https://lccn.loc.gov/2018009544

Cover and interior design: Sarah Olson
Front cover images: *Pride and Prejudice* book cover:
  Wikimedia Commons; Amber cross: Photo by Peter
  Smith, courtesy of the Jane Austen's House Museum;
  Quill and ink: 123rf.com; Fox hunt: From *The Cream
  of Leicestershire; eleven seasons' skimmings, notable runs
  and incidents of the chase*, selected and republished
  from "The Field" (1883); Chawton House: Courtesy
  of the Chawton House Library; Silhouette: Courtesy
  of the Chawton House Library; Steventon Rectory:
  Wikimedia Commons; Jane Austen: Wikimedia
  Commons
Back cover images: Statue of Jane Austen: Roger Utting/
  Shutterstock.com; Teacup: Dmitry Elagin/123rf.com
Interior illustrations: Lindsey Cleworth Schauer

Printed in the United States of America
5 4 3 2 1

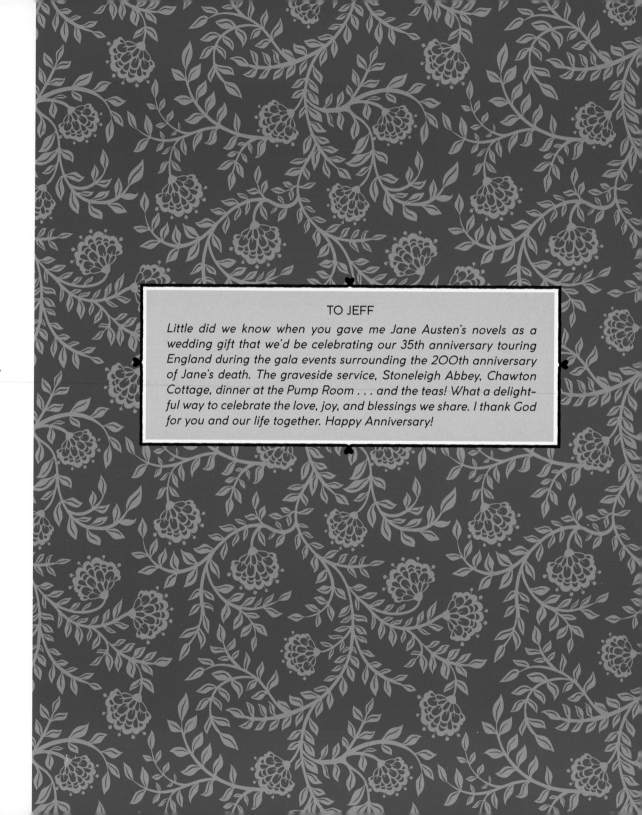

TO JEFF

Little did we know when you gave me Jane Austen's novels as a wedding gift that we'd be celebrating our 35th anniversary touring England during the gala events surrounding the 200th anniversary of Jane's death. The graveside service, Stoneleigh Abbey, Chawton Cottage, dinner at the Pump Room . . . and the teas! What a delightful way to celebrate the love, joy, and blessings we share. I thank God for you and our life together. Happy Anniversary!

CONTENTS

AUTHOR'S NOTE

The journey I took writing this book was a delightful challenge. Delightful in that so many Austen scholars and dedicated Janeites paved the way for me to follow in Jane's footsteps; and challenging in that there are limited primary sources available to draw from for facts about Jane. It was easier to quote Jane's own words from letters she wrote as an adult. For her earlier years, however, I gave Jane a voice at times by using dialog without quotes and written in italics. These instances are based on facts known about Jane in various circumstances but are not directly quoted, as limited information remains about her youth.

I also created an official website for this book that contains additional material that could not be included in a book of this scope or size. Please visit the *Jane Austen for Kids* website at www.nancyisanders .com/jane-austen. There you will find links to read all six novels online. Also featured are printable summaries of her juvenilia pieces "The History of England" and "Love and Friendship," as well as links to read these online. I've included links to videos of English country-dances popular during Jane's time: Juice of Barley, Hole in the Wall, and the Boulanger. You'll find a free educator's guide, online resources, acknowledgments, and a more complete bibliography. This site also includes photos from my tour of England in 2017, when the country celebrated the 200th anniversary of Jane Austen's death with gala programs, private tours, and special events.

TIME LINE

1752 Aunt Philadelphia sails to India and marries Tysoe Hancock

1761 Uncle Tysoe becomes business partners in India with Warren Hastings

1765 Warren Hastings and the Hancocks (with daughter Eliza) return to England

1774 Hastings is appointed first British governor of India

1775 American Revolution begins

Jane Austen born on December 16 at Steventon Parsonage in England

Jane Austen at her writing desk.
Photo by author, courtesy of the Winchester Cathedral

1783 Brother Edward is adopted by wealthy relatives

Jane is sent to Mrs. Cawley's school in Oxford with sister and cousin

Mrs. Cawley moves with Jane and girls to Southampton

British troops return from American Revolution to Southampton, bringing typhus

Jane catches typhus, nearly dies, and is sent home

1785 Jane attends Reading Abbey School with sister and cousin

1786 Jane returns home after ending formal education

Eliza Hancock de Feuillide visits Steventon Parsonage for Christmas

1787 Jane begins writing juvenilia

1788 Brother Francis sails to East Indies with the British Royal Navy

1789 Brothers James and Henry Austen publish *The Loiterer*

French Revolution begins

1793 Louis XVI is sent to the guillotine in France during Reign of Terror

Brothers Edward and James have first children; Jane becomes an aunt

Jane writes last of juvenilia

1794 Cousin Eliza's aristocratic husband sent to the guillotine in France

Brother Charles sets sail with the Royal Navy

1795   Jane begins writing *Elinor and Marianne* (to become *Sense and Sensibility*)

Jane dances with Tom Lefroy in series of Christmas balls

1796   Jane begins writing *First Impressions* (to become *Pride and Prejudice*)

1797   Brother Henry and Cousin Eliza marry

1798   Jane begins writing *Susan* (to become *Northanger Abbey*)

1799   Jane's Aunt Leigh Perrot accused of shoplifting but later acquitted

1801   Jane's father retires and moves the family to Bath

1802   The Treaty of Miens declares peace between Britain and France

Harris Bigg-Wither proposes to Jane; she accepts, then refuses

1803   Jane revises *Northanger Abbey*, then sells it to publisher

Napoleon breaks peace treaty; Jane's brothers Francis and Charles reenlist

1805   Jane's father dies in Bath

Martha Lloyd moves in with the Austen women

C. 1807   Jane, Austen women, and Martha Lloyd move in with Francis in Southampton

1809   Jane, Austen women, and Martha Lloyd move to Chawton Cottage

Jane rewrites *Sense and Sensibility*

1811   The prince regent officially begins rule during his father George III's illness

Jane begins writing *Mansfield Park*

Sense and Sensibility is published

1813   *Pride and Prejudice* is published

1814   Jane begins writing *Emma*

Mansfield Park is published

1815   Jane begins writing *Persuasion*

Jane stays with brother Henry in London during his illness

Jane visits the prince regent's library at Carlton House

Emma published with dedication to the prince regent

1816   Brother Henry buys back rights to *Northanger Abbey*

Jane finishes *Persuasion*

1817   Jane travels to Winchester for medical care

Jane Austen dies on July 18 and is buried in Winchester Cathedral

Northanger Abbey and *Persuasion* are published by Henry and Cassandra

1832   Publisher Richard Bentley purchases copyrights to Jane Austen's six novels

C. 1870   Nephew James Edward Austen-Leigh publishes a Jane Austen biography

Jane Austen. *Photo by author, courtesy of the Winchester Cathedral*

PRIDE

---✦※✦---

THE AUSTEN ANCESTORS

It is a truth universally acknowledged that Jane Austen's beginnings seemed simple enough. She was born in England on December 16, 1775, the seventh of eight children. Her family wasn't wealthy, but they were part of the gentry, the fortunate social class that owned land in Georgian England. The Georgian era lasted from 1714 to 1830, when England was ruled by four successive kings named George: George I, his son George II, George II's grandson George III, and George III's son George IV.

Steventon Parsonage, the home where Jane Austen was born, as sketched by Anna Austen Lefroy, Jane's niece. This drawing is thought to be slightly inaccurate regarding some details of the building.
Courtesy of the Jane Austen's House Museum

Statue of Jane Austen. *Photo by author, courtesy of the Jane Austen Centre in Bath*

Jane lived life surrounded by family, friends, and festivities. She loved to dance and merrily dance she did. Many of her joy-filled days were also spent in quiet pleasures: gathering flowers in English gardens and walking through the countryside. And the teas she enjoyed! Jane's life was rich in the delight of daily moments. She never married but shared a bedroom with her older sister, Cassandra, until Jane died at age 41.

Even as a teenager, Jane took delight in storytelling. Her childhood writings are still read today. As she grew older, she eventually wrote six complete novels. Four were published during her lifetime, but alas, they were released anonymously, so most people didn't know Jane had written them. After she died a quiet death from an unknown illness, her brother and sister published her other two novels. They included a note identifying their sister as the author of all six works.

Who could have guessed Jane would one day become one of the most beloved authors of all time? Many literary scholars hold up her works along with Shakespeare's as among the best in the English language and consider her England's most famous novelist. Fans throughout the world call her "our Jane." They read her books—numerous times—and join clubs to celebrate all things Jane, calling themselves "Janeites." Movies, television series, and books (both nonfiction and fiction) based on her novels and her life are wildly popular.

To many, Jane Austen truly *is* a heroine. Living when women had limited opportunities, little education, and few privileges, she engaged in the witty occupation of writing. She wrote and rewrote her novels until they shone. She studied human characteristics and the complicated social etiquette of her times, identifying universal emotions that readers relate to even now.

Our Jane. Everything Jane. Clever, witty, high-spirited, and kindhearted Jane. What was it that made her so special both during her life and to so many of us today?

THE GENTRY

George Austen, Jane's father, was born in Tonbridge in the county of Kent, England, in 1731. The Austen ancestors were in the woolen industry. Known as clothiers, they provided sheep's wool to weavers, who made cloth. The Austens then sold this cloth to merchants.

Because of their gray livery (the jackets their coachmen wore), the Austens "were usually called the Gray Coats of Kent." By the time George was born, they had become gentry, the fortunate social class that owned land in Georgian England. The Austen family was so large that their combined votes counted heavily on election day. They were therefore a strong influence on the politics in the area where they lived.

George's father, William Austen, married a widow. She had a son, William Walter, from her first marriage. Together, George's father and mother had three children: Philadelphia, George, and Leonora. Sadly their mother died when the children were still young. Three years later their father married again, but he died a year after that. After this, their stepmother would have nothing to do with the children. She sent them to live with family members. It was a sorrowful beginning for six-year-old George and his siblings, who were now penniless orphans. William Walter, George's half brother, went to live with his mother's relatives. George, Philadelphia, and Leonora landed in London with their father's brother.

After a short time in London, George's aunt Betty took him under her wing. He moved to Betty and her husband's home back in Tonbridge.

Another uncle, Francis Austen, paid for George's education. Such an arrangement was not uncommon in Georgian England. Wealthy members of ancient families took pride in providing for their less fortunate relatives. This was partly to keep the grand estates they owned within the family.

Young George was a clever lad. When he was 16, he won a scholarship to attend St. John's College at Oxford University. As a member of the gentry, his choices for a "respectable" career were limited to becoming a clergyman or joining the military. All other trades or businesses were not considered worthy of the gentry class in Georgian England.

"A person may be proud without being vain. Pride relates more to our opinion of ourselves, vanity to what we would have others think of us."
—*Pride and Prejudice*

Host a Regency Tea

Drinking tea was an everyday part of Jane's life. And the parties where tea was served were elegant! "We drank tea again yesterday with the Tilsons, and met the Smiths. I find all these little parties very pleasant," Jane wrote in a letter to her sister Cassandra. One of Jane's household responsibilities was to purchase the tea. When she visited London, she shopped at Twinings, a tea shop still open today, where she probably bought black or green tea imported from China.

Thomas and Catherine Knight, Jane's relatives who adopted Jane's brother Edward, had a family cookbook. Jane probably enjoyed these recipes served during her visits to Edward's estate, Godmersham Park in Kent, or at another of his homes, Chawton House in Hampshire. Chawton was often referred to as the "Great House." In a letter to her niece Anna, Jane shared that she had spent the previous night "drinking tea at the Great House."

ADULT SUPERVISION REQUIRED

Now it's your turn to host a tea such as Jane would have enjoyed during the Regency period. (These were the years the Prince of Wales ruled as prince regent while his father, George III, was too ill to reign.)

Most important, be sure to include tea. Boil a pot of hot water, then steep or soak in the water the number of teabags recommended on the package. Use caffeine-free tea such as cinnamon apple, mint, or raspberry. Discard the teabags before pouring the tea into teacups. Offer honey or sugar cubes, along with milk or cream, if guests want to flavor their tea.

Also prepare sandwiches, cakes, and sweets. Teatime in Jane's day included delicacies like lemon pudding, macaroons, and gooseberry tarts. Tea drinkers also enjoyed rout cakes, cookies flavored with edible rose water and served at a rout, or "fashionable evening party."

The Knight family was fond of gingerbread and ginger cake. Their cookbook

> **"I would rather have nothing but tea."**
> **–from *Mansfield Park***

At Twinings tea shop, a storefront sign from 1787 remains today. The two Chinese figures informed customers that in Georgian England, all imported tea arrived from China. *Photo by author, courtesy of Twinings & Co.*

contains four of their favorite recipes. Here is a ginger cake recipe, inspired by one in the *The Knight Family Cookbook*, that you can bake for your Regency tea.

Ginger Cake

INGREDIENTS

1 cup softened margarine or butter

1 cup honey

4 egg whites

¾ cup hot water

1½ teaspoons ginger

1 teaspoon cinnamon

½ teaspoon nutmeg

2½ cups whole wheat pastry flour or white flour

MATERIALS

13-by-9-inch baking pan, greased

Large mixing bowl

Electric mixer

Toothpick (optional)

1. Preheat oven to 350°F and grease a 13-by-9-inch baking pan.

2. With an electric mixer, cream margarine (or butter) and honey in a large mixing bowl.

3. Add egg whites to the margarine and honey mixture and beat until well mixed.

4. Slowly pour hot water into the mixture, then add spices and beat well.

5. Gradually add flour, mixing on a low speed, then beat for one minute.

6. Pour batter into the greased baking pan and bake at 350°F for 35 minutes. (Insert toothpick to see if the cake is done—the toothpick should come out clean.)

7. Allow the cake to cool completely, and then cut into small squares and serve.

Tea table at Stoneleigh Abbey, where Jane visited her well-to-do relatives on her mother's side of the family. *Photo by author, courtesy of the Trustees of Stoneleigh Abbey*

Teapot with a box of loose tea. *Photo by author, courtesy of the Jane Austen Centre in Bath*

Design a Coat of Arms

The Austen family coat of arms. Its motto is written in Latin and reads, *Qui Invidet Minor Est*, **which means, "He who envies is inferior."** *Courtesy of the Jane Austen's House Museum*

The coat of arms, or "arms," were a matter of family pride. Only British gentry or families of distinction were allowed to own a coat of arms. These arms were displayed on the family's carriage so people could quickly identify who rode inside. The arms could be used in other ways. George Austen proudly printed his on bookplates, labels he put inside his books.

The background was typically the shape of a shield, but various shapes could be chosen. Unmarried daughters like Jane would display her family's arms on a diamond shape, or lozenge. The shield could be one solid color or divided into parts.

Pictures placed on the shield were called charges. Any symbol could be used, such as birds, fish, and reptiles, or castles, crowns, and hunting horns. Some images were a playful twist on the family name. Each had a motto, a phrase that held special meaning. Oftentimes the motto would contain a pun or witty reference to the family's name.

MATERIALS

- 🌺 Pencil
- 🌺 Poster board
- 🌺 Ruler
- 🌺 Crayons, markers, or paints
- 🌺 Scissors
- 🌺 Glue
- 🌺 Optional: Computer, color scanner, art program, and specialty paper

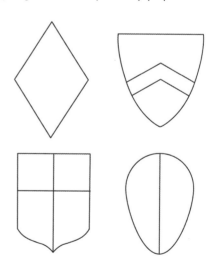

1. Choose the shape for your shield. Draw it on poster board, using a ruler to make sure the lines are straight. Leave it as one solid piece or divide it up.

2. Color the background. Here are the frequently used colors, along with their common names and symbolic meanings:

   Or (gold or yellow): generosity, wisdom

   Argent (silver or white): truth, purity, peace

   Sable (black): constancy, grief

   Azure (blue): loyalty, faith

   Gules (red): warrior, martyr, strength

   Vert (green): joy, hope, love

   Purpure (purple): royalty, sovereignty, justice

3. Pick the charges you want. Choose symbols that are meaningful to you or that play on your name. You can draw them yourself, cut them from magazines, or print them from the internet. Glue the charges to your shield.

4. Think of a catchy phrase to use as your motto, and add it your arms. You can also add more decorations. Some arms have symbols sitting on top called a crest. Others feature symbols on either side called supporters.

   You can display your coat of arms as is or use it to create bookplates, like George Austen's. Scan your coat of arms using a color scanner and upload the image to an art program or a blank word-processing document. Shrink its size and copy it so four images fit on one page. Type your name at the bottom of each. Print out several copies of this page, and cut apart the bookplates. Use an acid-free glue stick to attach a bookplate to the inside front page of your books.

I declare after all there is no enjoyment like reading!

THE CHURCH OF ENGLAND

George and most of the Austens were Anglicans, members of the Church of England. As Anglicanism was the national religion, the Church of England was very influential in politics and social customs. In George's day, gentlemen had to be Anglican to attend Oxford or Cambridge University, to work for the government, or to join the British military and become an officer.

At St. John's College, George earned multiple degrees. In 1754, he was ordained a deacon in the Church of England. The next year, he became a priest. By 1764, he was done with school and was ready to marry and start a family. But how could he support them?

His wealthy relations came to his aid. Uncle Francis knew George needed a rectory, a house where a priest lives to serve his parish, the people in the neighborhood surrounding his church. Francis purchased a rectory for George in the village of Deane.

In addition, Thomas Knight, a rich cousin, gave George one of the Knight estates. By the bye, this was a property that included a second, dilapidated rectory in the village of Steventon. One mile apart, both rectories were nestled in the county of Hampshire, which had scarcely 300 villagers.

(below) **St. John's College, Oxford.** *Courtesy of the British Library, Flickr Commons*

(right) **George Austen, Jane's father.** *Courtesy of the Jane Austen's House Museum*

At 33 years old, Rev. George Austen was a clergyman in charge of his parishioners' souls, baptisms, marriages, and funerals. With the help of his rich relations, he had risen from penniless orphan to the lower ranks of the gentry.

All he wanted now was a wife.

"It is a truth universally acknowledged, that a single man in possession of a good fortune, must be in want of a wife."

–Pride and Prejudice

THE DISTINGUISHED LEIGH FAMILY

George Austen courted Cassandra Leigh, the youngest daughter of Rev. Thomas Leigh. Young Cassandra Leigh was born into a family connected to English nobility. A distant ancestor was the Lord Mayor of London during the reign of Queen Elizabeth I. Other ancestors married wealthy aristocrats. The Leigh family was proud of their heritage. Cassandra was named after her great aunt Cassandra Willoughby, the Duchess of Chandos.

Cassandra's uncle, Dr. Theophilus Leigh, was master (or head) of Balliol College. College students, family members, and neighbors shared stories of the clever puns he told. Like her uncle, Cassandra was known for her puns.

(left) **Stoneleigh Abbey was owned by the Leighs, relatives on Mrs. Austen's side. In 1806, Jane visited Stoneleigh Abbey with her mother. Jane referred to it as "one of the finest Estates in England."** *Photo by author, courtesy of the Trustees of Stoneleigh Abbey*

(above) **Two hundred years before Jane Austen was born, her mother's ancestor Sir Thomas Leigh served as the distinguished Lord Mayor of London during the reign of Elizabeth I in 1558.** *Library of Congress, LC-USZ62-47605*

Learn Social Etiquette Among the Gentry

As a member of the landed gentry, George Austen would have been expected to know the basic rules of social etiquette and manners. You can learn some of these rules so you can practice them during a Regency tea or a ball.

INTRODUCTIONS

Manners for meeting and greeting another person were very important. You were never supposed to start talking with someone you didn't know. At a ball, the master of ceremonies introduced strangers to each other, especially gentlemen and young ladies so they could dance. When a gentleman strolled down the street past a young lady, if he did not know her very well he had to wait for her to bow to him before he could tip his hat at her. A man had to wait for a young woman to speak first.

CHAPERONING

A young lady was never supposed to walk through town by herself. Her governess (like a nanny), servant, sisters, or a gentleman must accompany her. If she was unmarried, she wasn't supposed to walk alone with a gentleman.

COMING OUT

When a girl turned 16, it was her turn for coming out, a term used to describe a young woman's formal entry to society. Before that, she was expected to behave quietly in a group of people, not speak to gentlemen in public, and not attend public balls. A young lady's time of coming out was very important. The event was often celebrated with an elegant ball.

Edward Austen Knight's dining table at Chawton House. *Photo by author, courtesy of the Chawton House Library*

DANCING

If a young lady was seated at a ball and a gentleman had no dance partner, he was expected to ask her to dance. If a gentleman asked a lady to reserve a specific dance for him, he was expected to arrive promptly. When a couple danced, it was considered rude to interrupt them. When a gentleman danced the last dance before supper with a lady, he was expected to sit with her during the meal. A gentleman was not supposed to dance more than two dances with the same lady unless he meant to ask her to marry him.

Clever, witty Cassandra and bright, educated George made a fine match. The couple married on April 26, 1764, at St. Swithin's, a church in the town of Bath.

George and Cassandra settled in the village of Deane. They had a student boarding with them named George Hastings. This little boy was the son of Warren Hastings, an English businessman turned politician in India. Warren Hastings was a business partner with George Austen's sister Philadelphia and her husband, Tysoe Hancock.

Young George Hastings was born in India but sent to England for his education. Alas! little George didn't fare well in England. Sadly, he caught a condition known as the "putrid sore throat" and died.

MOVING DAY

For several years, Cassandra and George rented the parsonage in Deane while the one at Steventon was being repaired. Their family grew. Sons James, George, and Edward were born within three years.

When the Steventon parsonage was finally ready, movers loaded up a wagon with the Austens' furniture, hefting the feather bed atop the load. Cassandra was not feeling well. Rather than

(left) **St. Swithin's Church.** *Photo by author, courtesy of St. Swithin's Church*

(above) **Jane Austen was born in 1775, the same year British soldiers fought with American colonists in the village of Lexington outside Boston, Massachusetts. This battle marked the start of the American Revolution.** *Library of Congress, LC-DIG-ppmsca-39753*

Play with Puns

Cassandra Austen, her ancestors, and her children were well known for their love of wordplay and puns. What is a pun? It's a word or phrase used in a clever way so as to have a double meaning.

Playing with puns is fun. If you learn how to "pun"ish your audience to get laughs, you'll be joining the ranks of literary giants such as William Shakespeare and Jane Austen. Both loved to sprinkle stories with witty wordplays.

Start by collecting puns. In Jane's day, people collected puns and wordplays in a scrapbook. Harriet Smith, in Jane Austen's book *Emma*, decorated the pages of her collection with ciphers—messages written in secret code. You can write your collection by hand or print them from your computer and glue them into your scrapbook.

Next, learn how to create your own puns. Here's how to get started.

1. Look online or in dictionaries and the-sauruses for homophones, homonyms, and homographs. Collect lists of these words and their meanings—you will need to know the definitions to create puns.

   Homophones are spelled differently but sound the same. For example: *gnu, new,* and *knew.*

   Homonyms are spelled and pronounced the same but have different meanings. For example, a *rose* is a flower, but *rose* is also the word used for getting up (The sun *rose* in the sky).

   Homographs are spelled the same but pronounced differently and have different meanings. For example, the *wind* blew in the trees, but you *wind* your clock.

2. Ask friends, family, and classmates to share their favorite sayings and proverbs. Collect these common phrases.

3. Use a rhyming dictionary to look up rhymes or near-rhymes for words you want to use in creating a pun.

4. Now put your research together. Choose words that have a double meaning and use them to write a clever sentence or phrase. Start with a common cliché or proverb and switch one or more words with words that rhyme or nearly rhyme to create a humorous twist.

Here are examples of puns:

This bag of coins shows the change in our society. (The word *change* has a double meaning that refers to coins as well as new events.)

I wondered why the ball kept getting bigger, and then it hit me. (The word

Cassandra (Leigh) Austen, Jane's mother. *Courtesy of the Jane Austen's House Museum*

hit has a double meaning that refers to the ball as well as an idea.)

You'll never be lonely in St. Louis because Missouri loves company. (This pun is based on the proverb "Misery loves company," with the word *misery* replaced by the near-rhyme *Missouri*.)

When Jane Austen was a girl, she wrote "A Beautiful Description of the Different Effects of Sensibility on Different Minds," a story featuring a doctor who speaks with puns. Notice how he uses the homophones *weak* and *week* in the following passage from Jane's juvenilia, *Volume the First*:

> *"In these situations we were this morning surprized by receiving a visit from Dr. Dowkins; 'I am come to see Melissa,' said he. 'How is She?'*
>
> *'Very weak indeed,' said the fainting Melissa.*
>
> *'Very weak,' replied the punning Doctor, 'aye indeed it is more than a very week since you have taken to your bed.'"*

The more puns you collect and try to write, the better you'll get at creating them. Perhaps you can write your own story about a character who speaks in puns.

walk the mile over the deeply rutted road to Steventon, she climbed onto the wagon. Cassandra rode high on the feather mattress like a queen riding in her royal carriage.

THE FAMILY GROWS

The Austen family continued to grow after they moved to Steventon. Henry was the next to arrive. He was followed by a baby girl named Cassandra. After that came another boy, named Francis.

On April 19, 1775, the British Army and a small group of American minutemen clashed in what came to be known as the Battles of Lexington and Concord, across the Atlantic Ocean in the colony of Massachusetts. The American Revolution was underway. By December, George III prepared to close American ports to commerce and trade. The Royal Navy, the most powerful force around the globe, prowled the seas like hungry sharks hunting their prey.

In Steventon, December blew in with icy winds. Mrs. Austen was nearing the full term of a pregnancy. She had written to her sister-in-law, Susannah Walter, "We are all, I thank God, in good health, and I am more nimble and active than I was last time, expect to be confined some time in November." November had come and gone, however, and no baby.

On December 16, 1775, Mrs. Austen's time of lying-in arrived; in the Georgian period, before modern hospitals, women usually stayed in bed for days or weeks after having a child. A baby girl

The Walters

William Walter, George's half brother, was 10 years older than George. They were separated when their father died, yet remained close. When William grew up, he married Susannah. Together the Walters had a number of children, including their daughter Philadelphia. They nicknamed her Phylly. Phylly was 14 years older than her cousin Jane. The Walters wrote frequent letters and kept many letters they received from the Austens. Today, these letters provide important information about Jane's early years.

was born, the Austens' second daughter. Her parents named her Jane and nicknamed her Jenny.

Mr. Austen wrote to his sister-in-law, Susannah:

Dear Sister,

You have doubtless been for some time in expectation of hearing from Hampshire, and perhaps wondered a little we were in our old age grown such bad reckoners, but so it was, for Cassy certainly expected to have been brought to bed a month ago; however, last night the time came, and without a great deal of warning, everything was soon happily over. We have now another girl, a present plaything for her sister Cassy, and a future companion. She is to be Jenny, and seems to me as if she would be as like Harry as Cassy is to Neddy. Your sister, thank God, is pure well after it.

When the new baby was one day old, Mr. Austen baptized her at home. For the next few months Jane stayed indoors away from icy drafts, snugly wrapped. Finally a sunny spring Sunday arrived. On April 5, 1776, Jane was carried to church, where her father christened her according to the tradition of the Church of England.

The Austens followed a local custom with each of their babies. After a few months at home, they settled the infant in a cottage with one of the villagers. One or both parents visited the baby every day. Sometimes if the weather was good enough, the neighbor would bring the baby to Steventon Parsonage to visit.

Jane was probably sent to a local nurse as her brothers and sister had been. She returned home when she was about two. Steventon Parsonage was the "cradle of genius" that shaped young Jane in her growing years.

Philadelphia Austen Hancock (1730-1792)

Philadelphia was George Austen's older sister. She grew up in London with their uncle Stephen and his wife. In 1745, Philadelphia, then 15, was apprenticed to a milliner in a part of London called Covent Garden. She learned how to make bonnets and work with lady's fashions. Her apprenticeship lasted five years. But what then? Young women had few opportunities. A life of poverty stared her in the face.

In 1752, acting with boldness as well as self-determined courage, Philadelphia set sail to India. Scholars are unsure whether Philadelphia traveled the dangerous journey alone or with a companion, but her goal seemed obvious. In India there were many British military and businessmen but few English women. After six months living abroad, Philadelphia married Tysoe Hancock. Now her future looked secure.

The Hancocks settled in India. Tysoe was a surgeon at Fort St. David, a British trading post of the East India Company. Several years later they moved to Calcutta, where Tysoe became a business partner with Warren Hastings, a clerk and rising politician working for the East India Company.

The couple had a daughter, named Eliza, in 1761. Warren Hastings was Eliza's godfather.

In 1765, 10 years before Jane was born, the Hancocks and Warren Hastings sailed back to England. They remained friends and in business together for years. Their travels to India, financial concerns, political ties, personal joys and sorrows, and letters to each other often involved Jane and her family.

Covent Garden in London has changed somewhat since the days Jane's aunt Philadelphia worked there. *Photo by author*

PREJUDICE

A CLERGYMAN'S DAUGHTER

Steventon Parsonage was a busy place while Jane grew up. With so many brothers, the house and gardens were full of boys!

First there was her eldest brother, James. By the time Jane was about two, James was already a tall lad of 12. He often visited the shelves in their father's personal library. James devoured Shakespeare and other giants of English literature. By the bye, he wrote as well.

At 10, Jane's brother Edward was good looking yet small. Comparing Edward with the next-youngest brother, Henry, their mother wrote to Susannah, "Indeed

Edward Austen Knight at a young age, Jane's fortunate brother. *Courtesy of the Jane Austen's House Museum*

Francis was just 18 months older than Jane. Adventurous, he was as bold as a fox stealing eggs from a henhouse. He got into frequent childhood scrapes without minding the punishment.

Jane was the seventh child. A cheerful girl, she delighted in making up stories and playing games.

Charles arrived by the time Jane was three and a half. He was her youngest brother, the Austens' eighth and final child. Jane and Cassandra were excited to have a baby to play with. They affectionately called Charles, "Our own particular little brother."

Sadly, one of Jane's brothers did not live at home. George, the second oldest, was cared for by a family in the village. He did not seem to develop as other children did and suffered health problems that may have included epilepsy. Perhaps George was deaf and unable to speak. Jane's mother called him "my poor little George."

WEALTHY RELATIVES

In May 1779, the crunch of carriage wheels sounded on the gravel lane leading up to Steventon Parsonage. What a fancy carriage and fine team of horses pulled up! It was their wealthy relative Thomas Knight II. His father, also named Thomas Knight, was the relative who had placed Jane's father as rector at Steventon years ago.

The son arrived with his bride, Catherine. The Knights were driving around on a grand "bridal tour." The couple seemed to enjoy their visit. They found 12-year-old Edward to be particularly charming.

no one would judge by their looks that there was above three years and a half difference in their ages, one is so little and the other so great."

Henry was six years old. Always ready to laugh, he was Jane's favorite brother. Jane, like so many others, was spellbound by his captivating personality.

Cassandra, her only sister, was almost three years older than Jane. Mr. and Mrs. Austen hoped the two sisters would become best friends.

In those days, a newly married couple sometimes took a younger relative along on their honeymoon. It helped pass the slow hours driving over bumpy country lanes. Plus, some strangers staged silly celebrations or pranks on newlyweds passing through their villages. A companion along on the trip helped avoid this, since the presence of a third person looked like an ordinary group rather than a couple sightseeing on their honeymoon.

The Knights did not yet have a companion. Would Mr. and Mrs. Austen allow young Edward to accompany them? Jane's parents gave their consent. From the humble parsonage into high society—what an opportunity for Edward!

TUTORING BUSINESS

Soon after this, when Jane was nearly four, another brother left home. In 1779, 14-year-old James headed off to college. Along with working as priest in his parish, Mr. Austen had worked as a tutor for more than five years. His pupils studied alongside Jane's older brothers as they all prepared for college. Mr. Austen was their schoolmaster, and Mrs. Austen oversaw their meals and laundry. So that year, three or four boys would be moving back in with Jane's family after the summer holiday.

August arrived. Summer holidays were over. Mounds of freshly cut hay filled their barn. The carrier's cart arrived at Steventon Parsonage loaded with heavy trunks. The cart was unloaded and luggage was hauled through the door, up two flights of stairs, and into the attic.

Boys' voices filled the parsonage. One by one, they arrived like homing pigeons flying back to their roost. They took their familiar place in the crowded Austen household.

Young Thomas Fowle was probably there. His older brother Fuller was already a student. Their father was a friend of Mr. Austen and a classmate from his university days. More pupils came from other "chosen friends and acquaintances."

Jane's childhood was filled with the sights and sounds of learning. In her father's study, students peered through Mr. Austen's microscope at the miniature world found in a raindrop. Jane's father read aloud to his pupils from the classics as well as modern literature. The boys studied Latin grammar with occasional attempts at reading and deciphering the New Testament of the Bible in Greek.

JANE'S EARLY EDUCATION

Not much is known about Jane's early education. From her writings and the books that survive from her childhood, however, we can guess at some things. Most young girls learned at first from their mother. Mrs. Austen probably taught Jane her earliest lessons. Jane owned a popular children's book, *The History of Little Goody Two-Shoes*, which was published in London in 1765 by John Newbery.

The book taught a moral, or lesson. In the story, little Margery Meanwell and her brother Tommy are orphans. Poor Margery wears tattered clothes and has only one shoe. A kind clergyman and his wife take both children under their wing. Tommy is given clothes and sent to sea to become a sailor.

Jane loved and cherished her book *The History of Little Goody Two-Shoes.*
Internet Archive Book Images on Flickr from The Heart of Oak Books (1906)

This book also taught the value of education. Young Margery determines to learn to read by borrowing books. Then she helps other children learn their letters.

She found that only the following letters were required to spell all the words in the world; but as some of these were large, and some small, she with her knife cut out of several pieces of wood six sets as follows:

A B C D E F G H I J K L M N O P Q R S T U V W X Y Z

and ten sets of these:

a b c d e f g h I j k l m n o p q r s t u v w x y z.

And having got an old spelling book, she made her companions set up all the words they wanted to spell: and after that, taught them to compose sentences.

Margery is given a pair of shoes and money to buy clothes.

Margery is so happy to have two shoes instead of one that she tells everyone about it. They affectionately call her "Little Goody Two-Shoes." Because Margery is kind and helpful to others, she marries a wealthy gentleman and has enough money to continue helping others even more. The moral of the story is that if you are kind to others, you will earn your reward.

Jane also likely learned to recite poetry. Poetry was popular in Georgian England, and children memorized poems as part of their schooling. A popular poem from her time was "The Beggar's Petition" by Thomas Moss. In this poem, a man without any money or a place to live stops at a mansion. He asks for shelter and food, but a servant drives him away. The man then stops at another house and repeats his plea.

"The Beggar's Petition" was a much-loved poem and was published in many poetry collections. People bought portraits of the beggar and displayed them in their homes as if it were their family's coat of arms. Nearly every child in England was taught to memorize the stanzas.

Young children were also taught to recite famous fables, short stories or poems that had a moral lesson and often had characters that were animals. A popular fable at that time was "The Hare and Many Friends." This fable is about a hare, or rabbit, who thinks all the animals are his friends. However, early one morning, the hare hears the barking of hound dogs. (In Jane's day, gentlemen enjoyed hunting rabbits or foxes by sending a pack of hound dogs out to track the animal down. The men followed the hounds on horseback, racing over the fields.)

Alas! when the hare in the fable hears the hound dogs, she knows they are coming to catch her. She asks her animal friends for help. One by one, she asks each animal to let her climb up on its

The Beggar's Petition
by Thomas Moss (c. 1740–1808)
Selected Stanzas

Pity the sorrows of a poor old man,
Whose trembling limbs have borne him to your door,
Whose days are dwindled to the shortest span.
Oh! Give relief! And Heaven will bless your store.

These tattered clothes my poverty bespeak,
These hoary* locks proclaim my lengthened years;
And many a furrow in my grief-worn cheek
Has been the channel to a flood of tears.

Yon house, erected on the rising ground,
With tempting aspect drew me from my road;
For Plenty there a residence has found,
And Grandeur a magnificent abode.

(Hard is the fate of the infirm and poor!)
Here craving for a morsel of their bread,
A pampered menial† drove me from the door,
To seek a shelter in the humble shed.

Oh! take me to your hospitable dome,
Keen blows the wind, and piercing is the cold!
Short is my passage to the friendly tomb,
For I am poor and miserably old.

Pity the sorrows of a poor old man!
Whose trembling limbs have borne him to your door,
Whose days are dwindled to the shortest span,
Oh! Give relief! And Heaven will bless your store.

* *white with age*
† *servant*

> "[Catherine Morland's] mother was three months in teaching her only to repeat the 'Beggar's Petition;' and after all, her next sister, Sally, could say it better than she did. Not that Catherine was always stupid,—by no means; she learnt the fable of 'The Hare and Many Friends' as quickly as any girl in England." —*Northanger Abbey*

back. One by one, the animals make up excuses why they can't help. This fable taught children the true meaning of friendship.

LIFE AT STEVENTON

Jane grew up in a simple country home without the fancy comforts her wealthier relatives enjoyed. Steventon Parsonage was a plain, Georgian-style building with rows of windows across its front. On the inside, the rooms appeared small and humble. Jane's nephew (and biographer) James Edward Austen-Leigh explained how "the beams which supported the upper floors projected into the rooms below in all their naked simplicity, covered only by a coat of paint or whitewash."

Just inside the front door was a small parlor, or sitting room to welcome guests. Also facing out to the front was a second, roomier parlor the family used as a dining or common sitting room. The kitchen was on the right side, and Mr. Austen's study was at the back. Several other rooms were also at the back for the servants—even though the Austens were not wealthy according to gentry standards, they hired local villagers as servants and maids.

The second story boasted seven bedrooms for the Austens. There were also three attics on the third story. These served as bedrooms, usually for the students boarding with the family. Each year, however, Mr. Austen's pupils went home for Midsummer (a summer holiday) and Christmas. At these times, so many cousins or friends came to stay that the crowded house seemed as if it would burst at the seams.

When Jane was five years old, a coachman arrived at Steventon Parsonage on horseback, pulling a pony behind him—a surprise for Jane's brother Edward. Thomas and Catherine Knight sent a message along, too. Edward was invited to visit them at Godmersham, their grand estate in Kent. Mr. Austen hesitated. What about Edward's Latin grammar? When would the boy have time to study? Mr. Austen seemed to be strongly prejudiced against the idea. Mrs. Austen, however, knew this might be an opportunity that would shape her son's future as no Latin grammar could. She said, "I think, my dear, you had better oblige your cousins and let the child go."

Was it at that moment or a short time later that seven-year-old Francis announced that *he* wanted a pony of his own? He was determined to buy one, and so he did, for 1 pound, 11 shillings, and six-pence. Francis named his pony Squirrel.

Mrs. Austen made Francis a stylish new hunting suit by cutting apart her own red riding habit, a long skirt and jacket she'd worn on her wedding trip and during the early years of her marriage. Now Francis looked as smart as a British officer fighting for George III overseas in the war against George Washington and the colonists.

On the day of the foxhunt, away rode Francis on his pony. Henry and some of the boys likely rode any donkey or pony they could find. The other boys scrambled after them on foot. They all raced recklessly off to the hunting field. Daredevil Francis galloped among them in his bright-red hunting suit, "jumping everything that the pony could get its nose over."

Mrs. Austen oversaw the poultry and a dairy at Steventon Parsonage. As was a common practice among the gentry, she probably hired local villagers to feed the animals and milk the Alderney cows. She wrote to her sister-in-law Susannah, encouraging her to bring Phylly to visit: "Mr. Austen wants to show his brother his lands and his cattle and many other matters. . . . I have got a nice dairy fitted up, and am now worth a bull and six cows . . . and here I have got turkeys and ducks and chickens for Phylly's amusement." Jane's mother also grew a large vegetable garden during the summer.

Mr. Austen raised pigs, cattle, and crops at Cheesedown Farm, 200 acres of land near Steventon. Local laborers were hired to harvest the grains. In 1775, the year Jane was born, Mrs. Austen

Fox hunting. *Internet Archive Book Images on Flickr from The Cream of Leicestershire; eleven seasons' skimmings, notable runs and incidents of the chase, selected and republished from "The Field" (1883)*

wrote to her sister-in-law, "The wheat promises to be very good this year, but we have had a most sad wet time for getting it in, however, we got the last load in yesterday, just four weeks after we first began reaping. I am afraid the weather is not likely to mend for it rains very much today, and we want dry weather for our peas and oats; I don't hear of any barley ripe yet, so I am afraid it will be very late before harvest is over."

FUN AND GAMES

Jane loved to play games. Her niece Caroline once said, "[Aunt Jane] could throw the spilikens for us, better than anyone else, and she was wonderfully successful at cup and ball."

23

James Edward Austen-Leigh agreed: "Jane Austen was successful in everything that she attempted with her fingers. None of us could throw spilikins in so perfect a circle, or take them off with so steady a hand. Her performances with cup and ball were marvelous. The one used at Chawton was an easy one, and she has been known to catch it on the point above an hundred times in succession, till her hand was weary. She sometimes found a resource in that simple game, when unable, from weakness in her eyes, to read or write long together."

Bilbocatch, or cup and ball, was a simple toy. It had a handle with a small cup on one end. A ball was attached with a string. Jane enjoyed tossing the ball up in the air and catching it in the cup.

Spillikins was a game similar to Jack Straws or Pick-up Sticks. One player tossed the sticks into a tangled pile. Then each player took turns picking up one at a time without moving any others. If none of the other sticks moved, the same player continued. Her turn was over when she moved a stick she wasn't trying to pick up. The person with the most sticks won.

Sometimes Jane's sister visited their relatives, the Coopers, in the city of Bath. After one of these visits Mr. Austen left the parsonage to bring Cassandra home. It was a summer day, and Jane was at home playing with Charles.

Since it was the season for haymaking, Mr. Austen's horses were probably busy pulling the hay wagon. Jane's father hired a rented carriage called a hack chaise. Little Jane had an idea. Instead of waiting for Cassandra to arrive, she could take her younger brother along and meet Cassandra along the road. She would get to "meet the chaise, and have the pleasure of riding home in it."

Leaving the garden, Jane and Charles may have followed a hedgerow, the thickly planted bushes and trees that bordered the winding lane. James Edward Austen-Leigh said that "two such hedgerows radiated, as it were, from the parsonage garden. One . . . proceeded westward, forming the southern boundary of the home meadows; and was formed into a rustic shrubbery, with occasional seats, entitled 'The Wood Walk.'"

Jane and Charles reached the road. They probably walked a short while before they spotted the carriage. Nearer and nearer the horses clattered, pulling the hack chaise. Finally, the carriage jolted to a stop. Jane and Charles joined Cassandra and their father in the chaise, and the horses were off again, taking them all home.

(below) **Bilbocatch, often called cup and ball.** *Photo by Jeff Sanders, courtesy of the Jane Austen Centre in Bath*

(right) **The Austen family's set of spillikins.** *Courtesy of the Jane Austen's House Museum*

Plant an English Kitchen Garden

Jane and her family loved gardens! The kitchen garden at Steventon Parsonage was surrounded by a wall to protect it from brisk winds and hungry deer. Flowers grew among herbs and vegetables in a delightful array. And Mrs. Austen loved potatoes.

To plant a Georgian-style kitchen garden, gather supplies such as an apron, gloves, a shovel, a hoe, and a trowel. Kitchen gardens typically include edible plants—vegetables, herbs, and fruit trees and bushes—as well as some ornamental flowers and shrubs. You might consider planting heirloom seeds to give your garden an old-fashioned look.

To grow potatoes like Mrs. Austen, purchase seed potatoes at a gardening center, or buy organic potatoes at a grocery store. (Don't use regular potatoes as they are often sprayed with chemicals to keep spuds from sprouting.) Cut each potato into several chunks, making sure each has two or three eyes. The eyes are where the spuds will sprout. Place these chunks in a paper bag for two to three days while they dry out.

Potatoes grow well in a sunny spot with loose soil. If planting in the ground, choose a spot that gets six or more hours of sun each day. Dig up the soil and use a hoe to loosen it. Dig holes 5 inches deep, spaced 10 inches apart. Place each potato chunk in its own hole and cover with loose soil. If you want to grow potatoes in a pot, use a large bucket with drainage holes drilled in the bottom. Put a 3-inch layer of dirt in the bucket, and place two or three potato chunks on top of the dirt. Cover them with 5 inches of loose soil, and place the planter in a sunny spot.

Keep the soil moist, but not too wet. When the sprouts get 5 to 6 inches tall, mound up loose soil at the base of the leaves. If you see an exposed potato, cover it with loose soil. When the leaves turn yellow and start to die (after 8 to 10 weeks), your potatoes are ready. Gently pull them out from the dirt. Scrub them off and enjoy!

The garden at Chawton Cottage, Jane's adult home, features flowers and plants used for a variety of purposes, including fabric dyes. *Photo by author, courtesy of the Jane Austen's House Museum*

> "Some of the flower seeds are coming up very well. . . . Our young piony at the foot of the fir-tree has just blown and looks very handsome."
> —Jane Austen, in a letter to her sister, Cassandra

Master the Rules of Cricket

Cricket was a popular sport during Jane's childhood. The game was usually a boy's activity, but sometimes girls joined in the fun. Watch a cricket match on television or online to see how it is played.

WORDS TO KNOW

bails: two pieces of wood balanced on top of the wicket

batsman: person at bat

boundary: edge of the cricket field

bowl: to pitch the ball toward the batsman

bowled: when a batsman misses the ball and the ball hits the wicket, resulting in the batsman being out

bowler: person who pitches the ball to the batsman

cricket ground: oval grass playing field surrounding the pitch

over: a set of six times in a row that a bowler pitches

pitch: a rectangular area of very short grass where the wickets stand opposite each other and the ball is thrown to the batsman

stumps: another name for the sticks or wickets placed behind the batsman

wicket: three sticks or stumps behind the batsman with two bails balanced on top

wicketkeeper: person who stands behind the wickets and catches the ball if the batsman misses

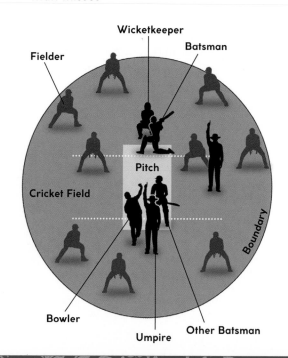

Wicketkeeper

Fielder

Batsman

Pitch

Cricket Field

Boundary

Bowler

Umpire

Other Batsman

HOW CRICKET IS PLAYED

1. A coin is tossed to see which team bats first. The team first to bat puts two batsmen on the field. The batsmen stand facing each other between the two wickets. They each stand directly in front of a wicket.

2. The other team chooses its first bowler. The rest of the team's players are fielders. The goal of the bowler is to hit the wicket with the ball. A fielder called the wicketkeeper stands behind the batsman's wicket to catch the ball if needed.

3. The bowler runs from behind his wicket and bowls the ball with an overarm throw to try to hit the other wicket. A bowler can bowl six times in a row. This set is called an *over*. After one bowler pitches an over, he takes a rest. A different player from his team becomes the new bowler and pitches from the other wicket.

4. The batsman guards the wicket by hitting the ball. If a batsman hits the ball and it bounces or rolls outside the boundary of the cricket field, the batsman automatically scores four runs. If the ball flies out of the field without hitting the ground, the batsman automatically scores six runs. If the ball stays in the field however, both batsmen run back and forth between the wickets to score as many runs as they can without getting out.

SOME RULES FOR GETTING OUT

1. If the bowler hits the wicket, the batsman is out.

2. If the batsman is hit by the ball because he blocked the wicket with his body instead of hitting the ball, the batsman is out.

3. If a fielder catches the ball before it hits the ground or goes off the field, the batsman is out.

4. If a fielder throws the ball and hits a wicket while the batsmen are running, the batsman nearest that wicket is out.

5. If a batsman gets out, a new player takes the place. The first inning is over after all 11 players bat on the first team.

6. The next team bats in the second inning. Each inning can last an hour or longer unless limits are agreed on.

7. The team with the most runs at the end of the second inning wins.

"[Catherine Morland] was fond of all boys' plays, and greatly preferred cricket not merely to dolls, but to the more heroic enjoyments of infancy, nursing a dormouse, feeding a canary-bird, or watering a rose-bush."
—*Northanger Abbey*

3

SENSE

>>◆>>

A LITERARY EDUCATION

Thomas and Catherine Knight did not have any children. When they died, who would be their heir and carry on their name? What was to become of their grand estate, Godmersham Park? And who would live at the beautiful Chawton House?

The Knights were so fond of Edward, they wanted to adopt him as their heir. So it was decided: when 16-year-old Edward finished his studies that year, he would join the Knights as their adopted son. He would eventually change his name to

Silhouette showing Edward Austen being presented to his adoptive parents.
Courtesy of the Chawton House Library

Chawton House, one of the estates Jane's brother Edward inherited.

Courtesy of the Chawton House Library

Edward Knight and inherit their money and property. Jane's parents felt it made sense to give their son this amazing opportunity.

FAMILY THEATRICALS

When Jane was young, her brothers performed theatricals, or plays. Her eldest brother, James, arrived home from college for Midsummer and Christmas holidays and brought home his passion for literature and the thrill of the stage.

Her brothers, perhaps with the help of hired workers, built sets of scenery—and for larger productions, set up a stage in the barn. There they could perform with a large cast. There was also plenty of seating for Jane and others to watch the performances. For smaller productions, the enterprising brothers took over the parsonage dining room. One of their earliest productions was *Matilda*, a popular play first performed at London's famous Drury Lane Theater in 1775, the year Jane was born.

Edward opened the show with a long speech, a poetic prologue written by James to introduce the five-act tragedy. The story took place during the era of William the Conqueror, king of England from 1066 to 1087. Two brothers, Edwin and Morcar, were in love with the same woman, Matilda, but Matilda loved only Edwin.

Morcar, determined to gain his prize, made the two lovers his prisoners and planned to murder Edwin. But when Matilda thought Edwin was dead, she vowed to join him in death rather than marry Morcar, much like the heroine in Shakespeare's *Romeo and Juliet*. At that moment, however, Morcar repented of his evil plans, and the lovers were happily reunited.

The Coopers

Mrs. Austen had an older sister named Jane who married a wealthy clergyman named Edward Cooper. The Coopers had two children, a son and daughter, each named after their parents. The family lived in Bath. Jane and Cassandra Austen were very close to their cousins Edward and Jane and stayed in Bath with the Coopers from time to time.

Sadly, Mr. and Mrs. Cooper died at an early age. Afterward, both Edward and Jane Cooper spent extended visits at the Austens'. Cousin Edward distinguished himself as a scholar, published author, and famous preacher. Cousin Jane eventually married Admiral Sir Thomas Williams at Steventon Parsonage and became Lady Williams. Charles Austen, Jane Austen's younger brother, served on several ships under Admiral Williams's command.

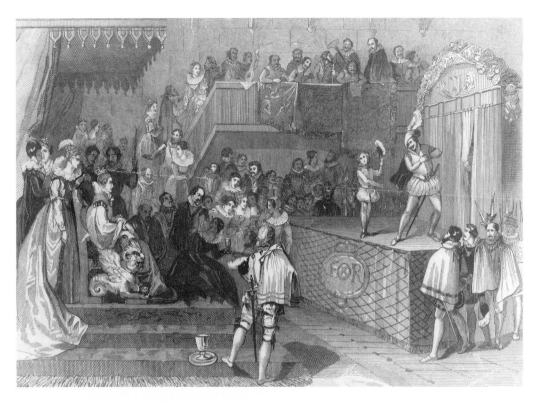

(above) **Shakespeare performing before Queen Elizabeth and her court.** *Library of Congress, LC-USZ62-116194*

(left) **James Austen, Jane's eldest brother.** *Courtesy of the Jane Austen's House Museum*

At the end, Thomas Fowle, one of Mr. Austen's students, stood up and delivered a grand epilogue, also written by James. What fine merriment indeed!

A Formal Education

Seven-year-old Jane was excited. Her big sister, Cassandra, and their cousin Jane Cooper were going away—and she was to go with them. Jane Cooper's aunt, a widow named Mrs. Cawley, opened a boarding school at Oxford, where she tutored 12-year-old Jane Cooper and 10-year-old Cassandra while little Jane tagged along. Unlike the easy openness of Mr. Austen's tutoring, Mrs. Cawley was a no-nonsense and "stiff-mannered" teacher.

One day a visitor was announced at the boarding school. James! A day of sightseeing was in store. James lived at Oxford while he was attending St. John's College, and he then continued there as a teacher, or fellow, until 1790. James was proud of England's famous college town. He took the girls to see the historic buildings he knew so well. Jane grew up in a house full of boys, but on this day, she saw older boys and young men everywhere. Dedicated scholars tucked themselves into quiet corners of university libraries, devouring books. Big boys walked through long halls on their way to classes. Young men recited prayers in dark, somber chapels. James showed his beloved Oxford to the girls as few outside visitors were able to experience it.

By the end of their long day, Jane was glad to go back to the boarding school, even to Mrs. Cawley's formalities. She later shared, "I never, but once, was in Oxford in my life and I am sure I never wish to go there again—they dragged me through so many dismal chapels, dusty libraries, and greasy halls, that it gave me the vapours for two days afterwards."

Jane's earliest experience at boarding school wasn't much to speak of. But things were about to get worse: Mrs. Cawley decided to move. In Georgian England, single women and widows had few options for earning an income, and many were confined to lives of poverty. Some in the gentry depended on financial help from family. Others took in boarders or became governesses. There were hardly any respectable jobs available for women.

Perhaps rent was cheaper elsewhere, or maybe Mrs. Cawley wanted a change. It seems she had money enough, left to her through an inheritance. Scholars have debated the reasons, but what is known for certain is that one day, Jane put on her

View of Oxford. *Courtesy of the British Library, Flickr Commons*

traveling bonnet and climbed into a carriage with Cassandra and Jane Cooper. Off they went with Mrs. Cawley and their trunks packed full with dresses and petticoats.

GATEWAY TO THE WORLD

The horses trotted south toward the sea. The carriage finally stopped in front of Mrs. Cawley's new boarding school, and Jane stepped out. The smell "of the stinking fish of Southampton" greeted them. Southampton, on the southern coast of England, was a port city where great ships sailed to and from faraway countries. It was often called the Gateway to the World. It was also a seaside resort to which people flocked in the summer to swim.

More than a century before Jane's arrival, in 1620, the famous ship called the *Mayflower* docked in Southampton and loaded supplies. The *Mayflower*, with its companion ship the *Speedwell*, originally sailed out of Southampton before turning back to Plymouth, England, because the *Speedwell* had sprung a leak. Finally, the *Mayflower* left Plymouth by itself and the Pilgrims sailed across the Atlantic Ocean on their historic journey to the New World.

Long after Jane's time, in 1912 the famous ship *Titanic* left port from Southampton. When the *Titanic* struck an iceberg and sank to the bottom of the Atlantic Ocean, the entire city mourned. Over 500 families in Southampton lost a loved one in the tragedy.

When Jane Austen lived in Southampton in 1783, an unexpected disaster hit the city. The Treaty of Paris had been signed on September 3, 1783, bringing the war to an end. British troops arrived home from the American Revolution. As boatloads of redcoats arrived back in England, the tired and wounded soldiers brought filth and disease.

A DEADLY DISEASE

Rat-a-tat-tat. Rat-a-tat-tat. The streets of Southampton echoed with the beating of the drum, the playing of the fife, and the marching of the king's troops. Soldiers and sailors were coming home after fighting in the American Revolution. These included sailors who had seen action against France and Spain aboard ships during the Siege of Gibraltar at the entrance to the Mediterranean Sea. Even though American troops had not been involved, it had been the largest battle of the Revolutionary War. One ship in particular brought not only soldiers but also something deadly. Sickness swept through Southampton like wildfire. It roared into Mrs. Cawley's boarding school and overwhelmed Jane.

Both Jane and Cassandra "were attacked by a putrid fever," which was probably typhus. What was to become of the little girls? People all over Southampton were dying, but "Mrs. Cawley would not write word of this to Steventon." Finally, Jane Cooper wrote a letter herself and dispatched it immediately.

After getting Jane's letter, "Mrs. Austen and Mrs. Cooper set off at once for Southampton." The two mothers sailed into Mrs. Cawley's boardinghouse like warships storming into port. They took the girls home.

Jane's great-nephew William Austen-Leigh and his nephew Richard Arthur Austen-Leigh (her biographers) noted, "Jane Austen was very ill and nearly died." Under Mrs. Austen's watchful nursing, however, both Jane and Cassandra got better.

Not so for the Coopers, unfortunately. Jane Cooper and her mother returned to Bath, but Mrs. Cooper had been exposed to the illness. She caught the putrid fever and died in October 1783. It was a sad time for both families.

A NEW SCHOOL

For nearly two years, Jane and Cassandra stayed within the safety of their family. Finally, however, Jane heard her parents talking about once again sending Cassandra to school with Jane Cooper. Jane felt miserable. Why did she have to stay home just because she was too little? She begged to go along. Mrs. Austen commented, "If Cassandra were going to have her head cut off, Jane would insist on sharing her fate."

So it was settled. The three girls would once again go to school together. Their parents chose the famous boarding school for young ladies known as the Abbey School. It was in Reading, about 25 miles northeast of Steventon Parsonage.

Nine-year-old Jane didn't write down memories of the Abbey School, but other students did. Her experience was probably very similar. Upon arriving, young girls were led into a cozy parlor in the front of the school. They would have

been introduced to and welcomed by the headmistress, Madame Latournelle. A grandmotherly woman, "she had never been seen or known to have changed the fashion of her dress. Her white muslin handkerchief was always pinned with the same number of pins, her muslin apron always hung in the same form; she always wore the same short sleeves, cuffs, and ruffles." The headmistress finished off her appearance with two bows. One was worn at the front of her dress with a matching one on her cap, "both being flat with two notched ends."

Even though her name was French, Madame Latournelle was no more French than Jane. She was English. To her young students, she must have seemed a mystery. Had she acquired a fake French name to attract wealthy parents? Or was she the widow of a French husband? Different sources suggested different ideas. One fact was certain though: Madame Latournelle could not speak a word of French! But the greatest mystery about Madame Latournelle to the girls was probably her artificial leg. No one knew how she lost her leg.

As a woman of significance who oversaw the education of daughters of the landed gentry, Madame Latournelle could afford to buy a prosthesis people called a cork leg. These artificial limbs were manufactured on Cork Street in London. The leg would have been made of wood, ivory, steel, and leather with a fake foot attached and would have moved and bent in a more natural way than the peg legs associated with the pirates hunted down by Britain's Royal Navy.

After meeting the headmistress and being shown to their rooms, new students settled into the daily routine at the school. Mary Butt Sherwood, a student at Abbey School five years after Jane, grew up to be a famous author too. Mary wrote about the school in her autobiography. She shared, "The liberty which the first class had was so great that if we attended our tutor in his study for an hour or two every morning . . . no human being ever took the trouble to inquire where else we spent the rest of the day between our meals. Thus, whether we gossiped in one turret or another, whether we lounged about the garden, or out of the window about the gateway, no one so much as said, 'Where have you been, mademoiselle?'"

There was much to explore! The Abbey School was in the gateway of the Reading Abbey ruins. Two magnificent staircases led students up above the gateway. At the top they could look out the window and see a field, the ancient abbey's courtyard that was used as a marketplace or country fairground.

Behind the gateway, the girls could climb a small hill and look down on the ruins of the abbey itself. The enormous Reading Abbey was built in the 1100s and had once been home to a community of Benedictine monks. This magnificent church was the third-largest and wealthiest abbey in England. Young ladies attending Abbey School took great delight in imaging ghosts haunting its crumbling turrets. What shivery tales Jane must have heard the big girls tell!

On hot afternoons, the girls played in the garden, sitting in the shade of giant trees. The

The inner gateway of Reading Abbey, part of the Abbey School when Jane Austen attended from 1785 to 1786.
Courtesy of Carol Taylor, artist

schoolhouse, a two-story brick building, was attached to one side of the gateway.

Jane spent about a year at the Abbey School. After morning prayers, students attended lessons. Jane and the younger classes were probably taught by schoolmistresses, while older girls learned from tutors. With a well-known boys' school nearby, there was a ready supply of instructors.

Young ladies were taught the art of letter writing along with simple arithmetic for household accounting. They also learned spelling, history, and geography. Jane practiced basic needleworking skills while older students completed entire embroidered landscapes. Music, drawing, and dancing lessons rounded out their formal education.

For holidays, school officials planned special events and performances. The elocution master taught eager actresses how to speak in theatrical productions. The dancing master directed the girls' steps in musical performances or ballets.

The Abbey School most likely had a French instructor as well. Speaking French was considered a mark of gentility. But Jane had another reason to be interested in learning how to pronounce *"Oui, madame,"* or *"Bonjour, mademoiselle."* Her aunt Philadelphia and cousin Eliza lived in France, and Jane was eager to meet these glamorous relatives who wrote gossipy letters to her family about Parisian high society.

HOME FOR CHRISTMAS

Christmastime arrived at the Abbey School. The students eagerly packed their trunks to go home for the holidays. When Jane and her sister reached home, their parents had no plans to return them to school. Jane's boarding school days were over. She turned 11 years old on December 16, 1786.

That Christmas, Mrs. Austen wrote a letter to her niece Phylly Walter about the holiday festivities at Steventon Parsonage:

We are now happy in the company of our Sister Hancock, Madame de Feuillide & the little Boy; they . . . will stay with us till the end of next Month. They all look & seem to be remarkably well, the little Boy grows very fat, he is very fair & very pretty. . . . We have borrowed a Piano-Forte, and [Eliza] plays to us every day; on Tuesday we are to have a very snug little dance in our parlour, just our own children, nephew & nieces, (for the two little Coopers come tomorrow) quite a family party. . . .

Five of my Children are now at home, Henry, Frank, Charles & my two Girls, who have now quite left school; Frank returns to Portsmouth in a few days, he has but short holidays at Christmas. Edward is well & happy in Switzerland, James set out for La Guienne, on a visit to the Count de Feuillide [Eliza's husband], near Eight weeks ago, I hope he is got there by this time and am impatient for a letter; he was wind-bound some weeks in the little Island of Jersey or he would have got to the end of his long Journey by the beginning of this Month.

Aunt Philadelphia and Cousin Eliza were recently arrived from France. Eliza chattered away in French, wore the newest Parisian fashions, and copied the free-spirited French customs. It was a shocking contrast from the morals and etiquette Jane was taught growing up in the home of an English clergyman.

Jane watched Eliza, whose husband had stayed behind at their château in France, flirt openly with her brother Henry. At 29 years old, Eliza seemed delighted to win the admiration of her younger cousin home from his studies at Oxford. At 16, Henry was handsome and eager to please.

Craft a Christmas Kissing Bough

During Christmas many houses were decorated with evergreens. A kissing bough was made by wrapping evergreen boughs, holly, or ivy around a wire frame. Sometimes fruit, paper flowers, or candles were added. A sprig of mistletoe hung from the bottom. In some homes, the kissing bough was kept in the servants' quarters or kitchen. In other houses, the kissing bough was hung from a chandelier or doorway.

ADULT SUPERVISION RECOMMENDED

MATERIALS

- 8-inch foam ball
- Christmas ribbon, 2 inches wide, 2 to 3 yards long
- Craft glue
- Gardening gloves
- Wire cutters (optional)
- Artificial Christmas flower picks, or fresh evergreen cuttings
- Sprig of mistletoe

1. Center the foam ball on a length of ribbon about 2 to 3 yards long. Bring the ends of the ribbon together and tie it around the ball. Apply a small amount of craft glue under the knot to secure it.

2. Tie the ribbon tails together to form a loop for a hanger.

3. Wear gardening gloves to protect your hands. If needed, use wire cutters to trim the flower pick stems to about 4 inches. (Some stems might already be short enough.) If using fresh greenery, cut branches similar in size.

4. Poke each flower pick or evergreen branch into the foam ball as far as it will go. If the stem is shorter than 2 inches, add a dab of craft glue.

5. Continue adding to the foam ball until it is covered. Attach mistletoe to the bottom. Hang the finished kissing bough from a chandelier, the ceiling, or a doorway.

Learn an English Country-Dance

Jane Austen loved to dance the country-dances popular in Georgian England. She also practiced playing country-dance songs on her pianoforte. At times she played for family and friends while they danced. "Hole in the Wall" and "Juice of Barley" are two popular English country-dances, but it's not known if Jane danced these tunes. Here are the steps to "Juice of Barley," known in England since the late 1600s.

1. First, partners line up in two parallel lines facing each other, men on one side and women on the other. This dance works best with at least three couples, and any number can join in.

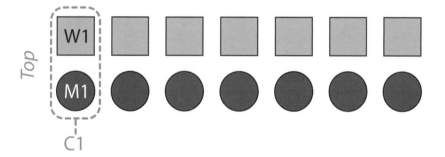

2. The couple at the top of the line (to the women's right) is Couple 1 (C1). The man is M1, the woman is W1. C1 makes up half of the first set of two couples. Count off sets of two couples down the line. If there is an extra couple at the end, they will not dance the first time, but will wait until C1 moves down the set. When they step into the dance, they will be Couple 2 (C2).

3. Start the music. Keep step with the music.

4. All partners (except the ones waiting out) step toward each other and then step to the left; pass around each other by their right shoulders, back to back; and step back into their original positions.

5. Partners hold hands, turn once around, and step back into their original positions.

6. Men step forward and do a half figure eight, stepping around the woman diagonal from them in the set. M1 leads the way and finishes in the next man's spot.

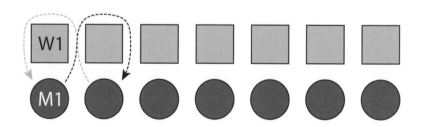

7. Everyone claps hands. All hold hands in their set of two couples and circle one time around. Women step forward and do a half figure-eight, stepping around the man diagonal from them in the set. W1 leads the way and finishes in the next woman's spot.

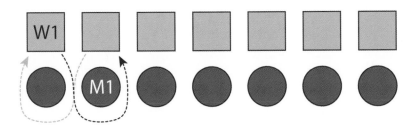

A ball at the Assembly Rooms in Bath. *Photo by author, courtesy of the Jane Austen Centre in Bath*

8. Everyone claps hands. All hold hands in their set of two couples and circle one time around.

9. C1 has moved one spot down the set toward the women's left. C1 starts to repeat the dance, still retaining their positions as M1 and W1 for the new set.

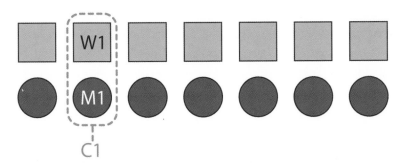

10. The new couple at the top of the line (to the women's right side) now waits out the dance until it repeats again. When they step back into the dance, they will now be C1 and move back down the line away from the top. The dance will be repeated, C1 moving down the set away from the top, until the music ends. If C1 reaches the other end of the line before the music ends, they become C2, turn around, and move back toward the top.

Eliza Hancock de Feuillide Austen (1761–1813)

Eliza Hancock de Feuillide Austen.
Wikimedia Commons

Jane Austen's father had a sister named Philadelphia. In 1752, Philadelphia sailed from London to India. Once there, she married Tysoe Hancock, who became a friend and business partner of Warren Hastings.

A number of years after Philadelphia married, she had a daughter. Gossip suggested Warren Hastings was the father. The baby was named Elizabeth in memory of the daughter Hastings had lost before his own wife died. Tysoe and Philadelphia chose Hastings as Elizabeth's godfather.

Betsy, as the little girl was called, lived in India until she was three. At that time, in 1765, Warren Hastings and the Hancocks sailed back to London. Back in England, Betsy met her Austen relatives for the first time. Jane was not yet born.

The Hancocks lived in London for several years. Their lifestyle was expensive, so Tysoe returned to India in 1769 to raise more income. Warren Hastings sailed back to India as well. Unfortunately, Tysoe died there in 1775, one month before Jane Austen was born.

Betsy grew up in London. Tutors came to her home and taught her French, music, and other subjects. She had a horse and enjoyed riding, although her father had his own reasons for providing this luxury. He wanted Betsy to ride for exercise and good health. Meanwhile, in a couple of installments around December of 1772, Warren Hastings deposited an impressive sum of 10,000 pounds in the bank for Betsy, making her a well-to-do young lady. By this time, she called herself Eliza.

Eliza and her mother left London, eventually traveling to Paris in 1779. They attended fancy balls and even dined at a grand party honoring Marie Antoinette and Louis XVI, the king and queen of France. Mother and daughter visited Versailles, the French king's glittering palace.

Around her 20th birthday, Eliza married Jean-François Capot de Feuillide, an officer in the French army. After Eliza became pregnant in 1786, she and her mother traveled from France to London for the birth of her son. She named him Hastings in honor of Warren Hastings, who had retired from politics and recently moved back to England. Once again, Eliza visited her relatives in Steventon Parsonage. Jane Austen was now 11 years old and excited to meet her dazzling cousin.

The French Revolution began in 1789. Citizens violently rebelled against their leaders and political system, which made returning to France dangerous. Eliza's husband, who still lived there, was condemned to die along with other French aristocrats during the frightening Reign of Terror. She lived the rest of her life in England. Her second husband was Jane's favorite brother, Henry. They lived in London, where Jane visited their glamorous parties and attended the theater with them.

Some scholars think Eliza inspired several characters in Jane's novels. The most notable is Mary Crawford, a young woman from London's high society in the novel *Mansfield Park*.

Every day, Jane gathered with the others around the pianoforte to listen to Eliza play. And to dance! Jane and the others were busy getting ready for the dance in their parlor the day after Christmas.

What a merry time to be home!

LEARNING FROM BOOKS

Jane's relatives left Steventon at the end of January and settled back in London. The older boys returned to Steventon Parsonage for their new school term. While we don't know what Jane did from one day to the next while growing up, she did write many letters when she was older. There are also diaries and letters family members and friends wrote, and historical accounts of the Austen family.

In the evenings on winter nights, candles lit up the room. Jane and Cassandra would sit next to the fireplace while snow fell softly outside. Under their mother's guidance, they practiced embroidery stitches or learned to sew shirts for their brothers. Their father's pupils lounged on the sofa and chairs. Mr. Austen read aloud to them all. He entertained his listeners with a wide range of books from classics in literature to the newest novels.

From now on, reading books would be a solid part of Jane's education. In reading about the worlds other people created in their poems, history books, and novels, Jane began to imagine brand-new worlds and stories of her own, even when she was as young as 12. She made up characters to inhabit those worlds.

And one day, Jane began to write down her stories.

> "Marianne, who had the knack of finding her way in every house to the library, however it might be avoided by the family in general, soon procured herself a book."
>
> —*Sense and Sensibility*

Decorate a Candle

Whether for reading by the fireplace, playing the pianoforte, or dancing at a ball, candles lit spaces everywhere in Jane Austen's day. You can make this decorative candle to celebrate Jane and her books.

ADULT SUPERVISION REQUIRED

MATERIALS

- Flameless LED wax pillar candle, white or cream color
- White tissue paper
- Scissors
- Ruler
- Printer paper
- Permanent markers, medium point
- Waxed paper
- Hair dryer

Jane Austen's signature.

Silhouette often attributed to Jane Austen. *Photo by author, courtesy of the Jane Austen Centre in Bath*

1. Cut a rectangle of white tissue paper to wrap around your candle. Trim it to leave a ½-inch space from the top and bottom edges of the candle and a ½-inch gap between the ends of the tissue paper.

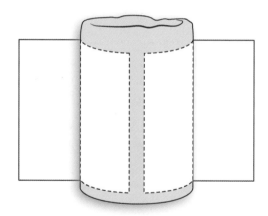

2. Place this rectangle on a sheet of printer paper and trace around it. The printer paper is your practice sheet. Set the tissue paper aside while you create the design.

42

On the printer paper, draw the design you want. You can trace Jane Austen's silhouette, write one of her quotes, or add her signature.

3. Place the rectangle of tissue paper on top of your design. Use permanent markers to trace your design onto the tissue paper, being careful not to tear it.

> "I never saw any thing equal to the comfort and style–Candles every where."–*Emma*

4. Cut a sheet of waxed paper that is at least 1 inch taller and 6 inches longer than your tissue paper.

5. Lay the waxed paper on your work surface, and center the tissue paper on it, with the design facedown. Place the candle on its side and center it in the tissue paper. Keeping the tissue paper and waxed paper in place, wrap them around the candle and grasp the excess waxed paper in one hand.

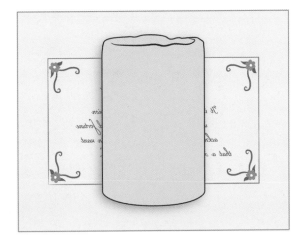

6. With an adult's help, hold the waxed paper in place and use a hair dryer to blow hot air onto the candle. This melts the waxed paper and seals the tissue paper onto the candle. Work carefully

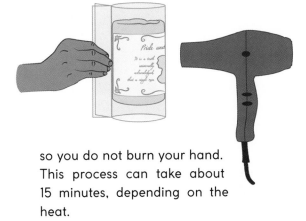

so you do not burn your hand. This process can take about 15 minutes, depending on the heat.

While working, you can occasionally turn off the hair dryer and remove the waxed paper. (Do not remove the tissue paper.) Gently test the edges of the tissue paper to see if it has been sealed to the candle. If needed, use a second sheet of waxed paper.

SENSIBILITY

<hr style="width:10%" />

YOUTHFUL WRITINGS

Make haste! Jane's thoughts seemed to compel her. *Write us down before you forget us!*

How diverting it would have been to be a robin on a branch outside the parsonage, peeking in to see where Jane wrote her earliest musings.

Alas! details explaining how, when, and where Jane wrote as a girl remain a mystery. But *what* she wrote can be read today, even in her handwriting. Her father gave her three notebooks, each with a cover of vellum, a leather used for binding books. Jane made a fair copy—a neat handwritten copy—of over 25

The Austens were fans of William Shakespeare. *Library of Congress, LC-USZC4-11465*

stories in these notebooks: *Volume the First*, *Volume the Second*, and *Volume the Third*. These notebooks are known collectively as her juvenilia—stories, poems, and scraps written while growing up.

For whom did Jane write? Was her juvenilia private, like a diary? Nay, her early writing was to be read by others. Most likely she read it aloud during family gatherings around a crackling fireside or on evenings when her father read aloud. We know this because of her dedications.

Jane dedicated her tales to family and friends. By the bye, she didn't just write someone's name. Jane's dedications were works of art in and of themselves. They ranged from simple to laughingly elaborate.

The first piece in *Volume the First*, "Frederick and Elfrida," is dedicated to her friend:

To Miss Lloyd

My Dear Martha,

As a small testimony of the gratitude I feel for your late generosity to me in finishing my muslin Cloak, I beg leave to offer you this little production of your sincere Freind [sic].

The Author

Jane's short novel "The Beautifull Cassandra" contains a gushing dedication to her sister, overflowing with sensibility, or emotional enthusiasm:

Dedicated by permission to Miss Austen.
Dedication:

Madam

You are a Phoenix. Your taste is refined, your Sentiments are noble, & your Virtues innumerable. Your Person is lovely your Figure, elegant, & your Form, majestic. Your Manners are polished, your Conversation is rational & your appearance singular. If therefore, the following Tale will afford one moment's amusement to you, every wish will be gratified of

Your most obedient
humble servant
The Author

It seems Jane found amusement when she wrote, even as a child. Some pieces were complete nonsense. In "Sir William Mountague," Jane introduces her hero with a hilariously long and rambling heritage:

Sir William Mountague was the son of Sir Henry Mountague, who was the son of Sir John Mountague, a descendant of Sir Christopher Mountague, who was the nephew of Sir Edward Mountague, whose ancestor was Sir James Mountague a near relation of Sir Robert Mountague, who inherited the Title & Estate from Sir Frederic Mountague.

When she wrote about another hero in "Memoirs of Mr. Clifford," she presents a humorously long list of carriages he owns—something her audience would find very amusing.

[Mr. Clifford] travelled in his Coach & Four, for he was a very rich young Man & kept a great many Carriages of which I do not recollect half. I can only remember that he had a Coach, a Chariot, a Chaise, a Landeau, a Landeaulet, a Phaeton, a Gig, a Whisky, an italian Chair, a Buggy, a Curricle & a wheelbarrow.

The characters in Jane's teen writings range from quaint to bizarre, silly to sinister. Among these, we catch glimpses of characters she would use in stories to come. Favorite names occur, such as Emma (in "Edgar and Emma"), Fanny and Elliott (in "The Mystery"), and Willoughby (in "The Visit"). Many names Jane chose can be found in her own family tree. Some of these names she would eventually choose for her published novels.

From her earliest writings, Jane's characters are her masterpieces. Each is cleverly unique. In the nonsense tale "The Adventures of Mr. Harley," a lengthy list of coach passengers becomes a joke: in just three paragraphs, Jane includes many characters and just as many laughs:

The Adventures of Mr. Harley

a short, but interesting Tale, is with all imaginable Respect inscribed to Mr. Francis William Austen Midshipman on board his Majestys Ship the Perseverance by his Obedient Servant The Author.

"For what do we live, but to make sport for our neighbors, and laugh at them in our turn?"
–*Pride and Prejudice*

A phaeton is a carriage such as this one from the early 1900s. *Library of Congress, LC-DIG-highsm-41260*

Samuel Johnson's Dictionary

Jane Austen admired Samuel Johnson and his literary achievements. On April 15, 1755, Johnson published his landmark *Dictionary of the English Language*. Even though his was not the first dictionary, it was monumental. Johnson's dictionary provided better definitions and included examples of how to use the words. These examples were drawn from sermons as well as passages from English literature.

Samuel Johnson. *Photo by author, courtesy of the Samuel Johnson Birthplace Museum*

As *witting*, I no other comfort have. *Shakesp. Hen.* VI.
WIT. *n. ſ.* [ƿꞇꞇepⲣ, Saxon ; from pꞇean, to know.]
1. The powers of the mind ; the mental faculties ; the intellects. This is the original signification.
 Who would set his *wit* to so foolish a bird ? *Shakespeare.*
 The king your father was reputed for
A prince most prudent, of an excellent
And unmatch'd *wit* and judgment. *Shakesp. Hen.* VIII.
 Will puts in practice what the *wit* deviseth :
Will ever acts, and *wit* contemplates still :
And as from *wit* the power of wisdom riseth,
All other virtues daughters are of will.
Will is the prince, and *wit* the counsellor,
Which doth for common good in council sit ;
And when *wit* is resolv'd, will lends her power
To execute what is advis'd by *wit*. *Davies's Ireland.*
 For *wit* and pow'r, their last endeavours bend
T' outshine each other. *Dryden.*

Johnson's dictionary was a two-volume project that took over eight years to create.
Photo by author, courtesy of the Samuel Johnson Birthplace Museum

---

Mr. Harley was one of many Children. Destined by his father for the Church & by his Mother for the Sea, desirous of pleasing both, he prevailed on Sir John to obtain for him a Chaplaincy on board a Man of War. He accordingly, cut his Hair & sailed.

In half a year he returned & sat-off in the Stage Coach for Hogsworth Green, the seat of Emma. His fellow travellers were, A man without a Hat, Another with two, An old maid & a young Wife.

This last appeared about 17 with fine dark Eyes & an elegant Shape; inshort Mr. Harley soon found out, that she was his Emma & recollected he had married her a few weeks before he left England.

Finis

CHRISTMAS AGAIN!

On December 17, 1787, one day after Jane's 12th birthday, her cousin Eliza and aunt Philadelphia headed to Steventon Parsonage to celebrate another Christmas. The Austens had been preparing for weeks. They sent out invitations to family and friends to stay with them at the parsonage for the holidays. The house was decorated. Smells of Christmas puddings and pies filled the air.

Jane's cousin Phylly Walter received her invitation but wasn't yet decided about going. "My uncle's barn is fitting up quite like a theatre," Phylly wrote to her brother about the Christmas festivities at Steventon, "and all the young folks are to take their part." Steventon Parsonage was as busy as a royal theater preparing to entertain George III. Eliza wrote to Phylly urging her to accept the invitation and join the fun.

> *Your accomodations at Steventon are the only things my Aunt Austen and myself are uneasy about, as the house being very full of company, she says she can only promise you 'a place to hide your head in,' but I think you will not mind this inconvenience. I am sure I should not—to be with you. Do not let your dress neither disturb you, as I think I can manage it so that the Green Room should provide you with what is necessary for acting. We purpose [sic] setting out the 17th of December. . . . I assure you we shall have a most brilliant party and a great deal of amusement, the house full of company, frequent balls. You cannot possibly resist so many temptations, especially when I tell you your old friend James is returned from France and is to be of the acting party.*

SPIRITUAL COMPASS

On Sundays, Jane joined Cassandra and the tide of family members flowing along the Church Walk. This was the Austens' name for the path from Steventon Parsonage to St. Nicholas Church. They walked up the steep hill behind their garden, following the lane between the bushes and trees that formed the hedgerow. Soon Jane and her family reached the church. Tall elm trees and old hawthorns shaded the crumbling tombstones in the church graveyard. Fragrant purple and white violets carpeted a sunny spot.

Jane and her family entered the ancient church. It stood in this secluded spot for over 700 years.

St. Nicholas Church, Steventon, Hampshire.
Photo by author, courtesy of St. Nicholas Church by kind permission of Steventon PCC

Perform a Theatrical

Jane's family's theatricals inspired her to write plays. One, "The Mystery," is part of her notebook Volume the First. *"The Mystery" is a short comedy and sounds faintly like Shakespeare.*

Theatricals at Steventon Parsonage were quite involved. You can perform "The Mystery" as a read-aloud play without props or costumes. If you want to perform "The Mystery" in true Austen style, however, you can make elaborate preparations.

THE COSTUMES

Your costumes can be from the Regency period. Ladies can make turbans to wear and curl their hair. The gentlemen can boast Regency-style side whiskers and make a top hat. (See pages 60 and 63 to make these costumes, and pages 90 and 92 for ideas on curling your hair or "growing" side whiskers.)

THE STAGE

A curtain can be made from a sheet or blanket hung on a curtain rod using clip-on curtain rings. The removable handle of a telescoping mop, broom, or garden tool makes a sturdy rod propped between two tall bookcases or stepladders that form the sides of a small stage.

The first scene takes place in a garden. You can use potted or hanging plants to decorate. Or you can paint a backdrop on butcher paper to hang. The garden at Steventon Parsonage, like most English gardens, had both vegetables and flowers growing

A gentleman and young lady. *Courtesy of Carol Taylor, artist*

alongside each other, as well as pathways. Giant elm trees grew along their garden wall.

The second scene takes place in a parlor. Two women are sitting, busy at their work. In Jane's day, this work could have been embroidery, decorating a bonnet, or hand-stitching a quilt. For this scene, set two chairs slightly facing each other. Provide props of hand-sewing.

The third scene takes place inside a house. A young man is sleeping on a sofa. Decorate the stage to look like an elegant sitting room in Georgian England. Arrange candles, old books, and trinkets on end tables next to a couch.

THE SCRIPT

Jane's oldest brother James often wrote additional material. He was known for elaborate prologues and epilogues written in rhyme. You can write a prologue to introduce "The

Mystery." You can also write an epilogue to wrap up the ending. Perhaps you would like to imagine what the secret might have been and "finish" Jane's unfinished comedy.

Be sure to give each character a copy of the following script by Jane Austen so that everyone can practice. Encourage everyone to act with great emotion and exaggerated sensibility.

THE MYSTERY

an unfinished Comedy.

DEDICATION

To the Reverend George Austen
Sir,
I humbly solicit your Patronage to the following Comedy, which tho' an unfinished one, is I flatter myself as complete a Mystery as any of its kind.
I am Sir your most Humble Servant.
The Author

DRAMATIS PERSONAE

Men	Women
Colonel Elliott	Fanny Elliott
Sir Edward Spangle	Mrs. Humbug
Old Humbug	and
Young Humbug	Daphne
and	
Corydon	

ACT THE FIRST
Scene the First
A Garden.

(Enter Corydon)
Cory: But Hush! I am interrupted.
(Exit Corydon)
(Enter Old Humbug & his Son, talking)
Old Hum: It is for that reason I wish you to follow my advice. Are you convinced of its propriety?
Young Hum: I am Sir, and will certainly act in the manner you have pointed out to me.
Old Hum: Then let us return to the House.
(Exeunt)

Scene the Second
A Parlour in Humbug's House.
Mrs. Humbug & Fanny, discovered at work.

Mrs. Hum: You understand me my Love?
Fanny: Perfectly ma'am. Pray continue your narration.
Mrs. Hum: Alas! it is nearly concluded, for I have nothing more to say on the Subject.
Fanny: Ah! here's Daphne.
(Enter Daphne)
Daphne: My dear Mrs. Humbug how d'ye do? Oh! Fanny, t'is all over.
Fanny: It is indeed!
Mrs. Hum: I'm very sorry to hear it.

Fanny: Then t'was to no purpose that I . . .
Daphne: None upon Earth.
Mrs. Hum: And what is to become of? . . .
Daphne: Oh! That's all settled.
Fanny *(whispers [to] Mrs. Humbug)*: And how is it determined?
Daphne: I'll tell you.
Mrs. Hum *(whispers [to] Fanny)*: And is he to? . . .
Daphne: I'll tell you all I know of the matter.
Fanny *(whispers [to] Mrs. Humbug & Fanny)*: Well! now I know everything about it, I'll go away.
Mrs. Hum and Daphne: And so will I.
(Exeunt)

Scene the Third
The Curtain rises and discovers Sir Edward Spangle reclined in an elegant Attitude on a Sofa, fast asleep.

(Enter Colonel Elliott)
Colonel: My Daughter is not here I see . . . there lies Sir Edward. . . . Shall I tell him the secret? . . . No, he'll certainly blab it. . . . But he is asleep and wont hear me. . . . So I'll e'en venture.
(Goes up to Sir Edward, whispers [to] him, & Exit)

End of the 1st Act
Finis

Villagers filed into the musty shadows and took their seats. Jane's own prayer gives a glimpse into her personal experience growing up as a member of the Anglican Church.

Jane believed her faith in Jesus Christ would save her from the punishment of sin and grant her eternal life after she died. She accepted teachings in the Bible as truth. These beliefs formed the foundation for her life. This faith was her moral compass and guided her in her personal life as well as in her writing.

The Golden Rule and the Ten Commandments were two of the most basic beliefs in her faith and at the heart of the Anglican Church. Based on Scripture found in the Bible in Matthew 7:12, the Golden Rule states, *Do unto others as you would have them do unto you.* The Ten Commandments, also found in the Bible in Exodus 20:1–17, list ten moral laws Jane would have been taught to follow:

The Lord is God. Thou shalt have no other gods before Him.
Thou shalt not worship carved images.
Thou shalt not take the Name of the Lord thy God in vain.
Remember the Sabbath day to keep it holy.
Honor thy father and thy mother.

(below) **This key is a replica of the original 15-inch church key.** *Photo by author, courtesy of St. Nicholas Church by kind permission of Steventon PCC*

(right) **It isn't known if Reverend Austen hid the church key in the hollow trunk of the ancient yew tree, but it was a local practice until 1975.** *Photo by author, courtesy of St. Nicholas Church by kind permission of Steventon PCC*

Thou shalt not murder.

Thou shalt not commit adultery.

Thou shalt not steal.

Thou shalt not bear false witness against thy neighbor.

Thou shalt not covet anything that is thy neighbor's.

In her juvenilia, Jane used humor to show what happened to characters who chose *not* to follow those basic principles, often with uproariously funny results.

Jane frequently used clergymen as characters. Since her father was a rector, she knew all about the everyday life of a gentleman rector. When her eldest brother, James, graduated from Oxford he became a curate, an assistant to the clergy.

One of her closest neighbors was also a clergyman. George Lefroy was the rector at Ashe, the parish next to Steventon. He lived with his wife, Anne, and their children in the Ashe Rectory, a grand house about two miles away.

Jane visited the Ashe Rectory frequently, sometimes to play with Lucy, who was four years younger. When Jane arrived at Ashe Rectory, Mrs. Lefroy greeted her with "genuine warmth." It seems that Mrs. Lefroy recognized something special in Jane, this "clever and lively girl."

Mrs. Lefroy talked with her bright-eyed, eager young neighbor about poetry, quoting most of the English poets by heart. They analyzed Shakespeare and other English playwrights. Together Mrs. Lefroy and Jane sang praises of Mary, Queen of Scots, their favorite member of the royal family.

Jane Austen's Prayer

Give us grace almighty father, so to pray, as to deserve to be heard, to address thee with our hearts, as with our lips. Thou art everywhere present, from thee no secret can be hid. May the knowledge of this, teach us to fix our thoughts on thee, with reverence and devotion that we pray not in vain.

May we now, and on each return of night, consider how the past day has been spent by us, what have been our prevailing thoughts, words and actions during it, and how far we can acquit ourselves of evil.

Have we thought irreverently of thee, have we disobeyed thy commandments, have we neglected any known duty, or willingly given pain to any human being? Incline us to ask our hearts these questions oh! God, to save us from deceiving ourselves by pride or vanity.

Give us a thankful sense of the blessings in which we live, of the many comforts of our lot; that we may not deserve to lose them by discontent or indifference.

Hear us almighty God, for his sake who has redeemed us, and taught us thus to pray.

Amen.

"We have all a better guide in ourselves, if we would attend to it, than any other person can be."
—*Mansfield Park*

Anne Lefroy (1749–1804)

The cultured wife of a well-to-do clergyman, Anne was affectionately known as Madam Lefroy. She believed in putting her Christian faith into action. Surrounded by villagers struggling under poverty, Anne determined to help. She opened a school in the elegant parsonage and invited children to attend, teaching them to read and write. She also taught the village women a cottage industry—work they could do at home—by showing them how to make small items from straw to sell.

A woman ahead of her time, Anne personally vaccinated more than 800 villagers against the dreaded smallpox. The new vaccine prevented the spread of this highly contagious disease known for its high fevers and skin rash that frequently resulted in death. As neighbor, mentor, and friend of the impressionable budding novelist Jane Austen, Anne Lefroy created a legacy that lived on. Many scholars think that Anne's characteristics and spiritual morals became qualities Jane wanted her heroines to achieve in her novels.

A view of the trial of Warren Hastings, February 13, 1788. *Library of Congress, LC-DIG-pga-02382*

FIERY TRIAL OF A FAMILY FRIEND

Jane's family had a friend in a high place. Warren Hastings, godfather to Cousin Eliza, had climbed the political ladder to become the first British governor general of India. A number of letters and papers survive that show the friendship between Hastings and Jane's family. Unfortunately, Hastings also had enemies.

In 1788, when Jane was 12, Warren Hastings faced a trial in London. He was impeached, charged with committing political crimes while in office in India. His accusers were led by Edmund Burke, Charles Fox, and Richard Sheridan, important political leaders and public speakers in that day.

Jane's cousin Phylly Walter attended the trial, probably along with Eliza and Philadelphia Hancock, in April 1788. In a letter to her brother, Phylly wrote that they "sat from ten till four, completely tired; but I had the satisfaction of hearing all the celebrated orators—Sheridan, Burke, and Fox. The first was so low we could not hear him, the second so hot and hasty we could not understand, the third was highly superior to either, as we could distinguish every word, but not to our satisfaction, as he is so much against Mr. Hastings whom we all wish so well."

SUMMER TOUR

Mr. Austen's uncle Francis was turning 90. The family planned a summer tour to celebrate.

Francis Austen was the rich uncle who had helped Jane's father by paying for his education and setting him up in Steventon Parsonage. The summer of 1788 seemed the perfect time to visit him at Sevenoaks in the county of Kent and celebrate his milestone birthday.

Uncle Francis's house was as busy as an inn undergoing preparations for a ball. There were puddings to make and meats to roast as everyone awaited the Walters: William; his wife, Susannah; and their adult daughter, Phylly. Almost before Jane knew it, they arrived. She had never met the Walters, even though letters frequently flew back and forth between the two families.

Cassandra, three years older, talked pleasantly with everyone. Someone mentioned that she and her older cousin Phylly looked alike—the pretty shape of their faces, their skin tone, even the way they walked and talked. Phylly herself noticed the similarity, and it seemed to please her.

But what of Jane? In a letter Phylly wrote to her brother, she explained what she thought about her younger cousin: "[She] is very like her brother Henry, not at all pretty & very prim, unlike a girl

Warren Hastings (1732–1818)

Born in England, Warren Hastings sailed to India in 1750 when he was 17, as a clerk with the East India Company. He became involved with politics. Warren's young son lived with the Austens in England and was tutored by Mr. Austen until the little boy died from illness. Warren Hastings was also the business partner and friend of Tysoe Hancock and his wife, Philadelphia, Jane's aunt and uncle. Warren became godfather and eventual financial benefactor of their daughter, Eliza Hancock de Feuillide Austen.

In 1772, Warren Hastings became governor of Bengal. From 1774 to 1784, he made influential decisions as the first British governor general of India. Political rivals accused Hastings of wrongdoing. He stepped down from his position and returned to England, where he faced impeachment.

The Austen family maintained ties with Hastings during his long trial, joining in dinner parties and social events as well as financial business. When he was finally declared not guilty in 1795, the Austens rejoiced at their friend's success. When Jane's book *Pride and Prejudice* was published in 1813, her brother Henry gave Warren a copy to read. Hastings wrote back to say he was pleased with the novel.

> "It is happy for you that you possess the talent of flattering with delicacy. May I ask whether these pleasing attentions proceed from the impulse of the moment, or are the result of previous study?"
> —*Pride and Prejudice*

Fashions worn by stylish gentlemen and ladies in Jane Austen's day. *Photo by author, courtesy of the Jane Austen Centre in Bath*

of twelve." Phylly gave one final conclusion, "Jane is whimsical and affected."

After several days at Sevenoaks, the Austens left for London to visit other relatives: Philadelphia Hancock; her daughter, Eliza de Feuillide; and Eliza's son, Hastings.

London! Jane had heard about London, but she probably had never yet been to "Town," as everyone called it. Perhaps she would get ideas for a new story.

The city of London was very different from life in the country. Gray smoke from thousands of chimneys hung over the busy scene. Most likely, the dirty city air made people's eyes sting. The smell lingered from countless chamber pots emptied into the sewers.

And the noise—*Hot cross buns! Fresh fish! Flowers!* cried the children, women, and men selling their goods along the crowded streets. Their voices rose together like an off-key chorus. They performed to the syncopated beat of the horses' hooves and the clatter of the hackney coaches, the hired carriages that darted back and forth.

On Bond Street, milliners' shops made turbans and bonnets. Pastry-cooks baked pastries in their shops. Young lords and ladies paraded by in their finery. Stylish men and women ate ices, a fancy dessert made with frozen cream.

Despite the dirt, smoke, and noise, London was exciting. Jane and her family arrived at 3 Orchard Street to visit with their relatives.

Eliza's son, Hastings, was now two years old. Sadly, he was showing the same symptoms that Jane's older brother George had shown before his parents had sent him to a neighbor's for care. Hastings was seized with convulsions at times. Most likely he was not walking or talking as he should for his age.

Cousin Eliza and Aunt Philadelphia were surrounded by "dust & litter and confusion" and were overwhelmed packing everything they owned and purchasing more besides. They planned to return to France, where Eliza's husband was waiting. But France had a dark cloud hovering over it. Revolution was in the air, and political unrest was stirring. The women wondered if it would be a safe place to live. Jane and her family tried to cheer up their relatives. After a short visit, the Austens headed home.

The air grew crisp. The garden behind the parsonage produced its last bounty of potatoes and vegetables. The leaves on the trees turned pretty shades of red and brown before falling to the ground. Noisy boys returned for the new school term. Jane continued her education along with Cassandra. They probably took lessons in drawing, singing, and playing the pianoforte from teachers who made the rounds visiting country homes to teach daughters of the gentry.

Twelve-year-old Jane continued her diet of reading Shakespeare, plays, poetry, history books, and novels. Also, she made one of her first attempts at writing a novel.

Her new story might have been written to remind her and Cassandra of the adventure of their first trip to London. It would be such a shocking and outrageous version filled with so much exaggerated sensibility that it would likely make Cassandra giggle at its absurdities.

"The Beautifull Cassandra" was twelve chapters, far fewer than the novels Jane read. To make this even sillier, each chapter would be only one or two sentences long. This short format itself would amuse Cassandra.

How could Jane entertain her sister best? She had an idea to create a heroine—named after her well-behaved sister—who behaved in the most ill-mannered ways possible.

The setting? London, of course.

The plot? Mocking the popular romantic novels of her day, Jane's heroine wouldn't fall in love with a noble young man. Instead, Jane's Cassandra fell in love with a bonnet, a fancy hat made especially for a wealthy lady. The rest of the story would be about the naughty things Cassandra did for an entire day, first stealing the bonnet and wearing it while parading by herself (without an escort—shocking indeed!) throughout London.

Quill pens and bottle of ink. *Photo by author, courtesy of the Jane Austen Centre in Bath*

"I am happier even than Jane; she only smiles, I laugh."
—*Pride and Prejudice*

The Beautifull* Cassandra

A NOVEL IN TWELVE CHAPTERS

Dedicated by permission to Miss Austen.

CHAPTER THE FIRST

Cassandra was the Daughter and the only Daughter of a celebrated Millener in Bond Street. Her father was of noble Birth, being the near relation of the Dutchess of —'s Butler.

CHAPTER THE 2D

When Cassandra had attained her 16th year, she was lovely & amiable & chancing to fall in love with an elegant Bonnet, her Mother had just completed bespoke by the Countess of — she placed it on her gentle Head & walked from her Mother's shop to make her Fortune.

Illustration of Cassandra wearing her elegant new bonnet. *Courtesy of Juliet McMaster, artist*

CHAPTER THE 3D

The first person she met, was the Viscount of — a young Man, no less celebrated for his Accomplishments & Virtues, than for his Elegance & Beauty. She curtseyed & walked on.

CHAPTER THE 4TH

She then proceeded to a Pastry-cooks where she devoured six ices, refused to pay for them, knocked down the Pastry Cook & walked away.

Illustration of Cassandra devouring six ices. *Courtesy of Juliet McMaster, artist*

CHAPTER THE 5TH

She next ascended a Hackney Coach & ordered it to Hampstead, where She was no sooner arrived than she ordered the Coachman to turn round & drive her back again.

CHAPTER THE 6TH

Being returned to the same spot of the same Street she had sate out from, the Coachman demanded his Pay.

CHAPTER THE 7TH

She searched her pockets over again & again; but every search was unsuccessfull. No money could she find. The man grew peremptory. She placed her bonnet on his head & ran away.

Illustration of Cassandra running away from the Coachman. *Courtesy of Juliet McMaster, artist*

CHAPTER THE 8TH

Thro' many a Street she then proceeded & met in none the least Adventure till on turning a Corner of Bloomsbury Square, she met Maria.

CHAPTER THE 9TH

Cassandra started & Maria seemed surprised; they trembled, blushed, turned pale & passed each other in mutual silence.

CHAPTER THE 10TH

Cassandra was next accosted by her friend the Widow, who squeezing out her little Head thro' her less window, asked her how she did? Cassandra curtseyed & went on.

CHAPTER THE 11TH

A quarter of a mile brought her to her paternal roof in Bond Street from which she had now been absent nearly 7 hours.

CHAPTER THE 12TH

She entered it & was pressed to her Mother's bosom by that worthy Woman. Cassandra smiled & whispered to herself "This is a day well spent."

Finis.

*This is the spelling Jane used in her original handwritten manuscript.

Create a Regency-Style Turban

The Regency period occurred around the early 1800s. These were the years the Prince of Wales ruled as Prince Regent in place of his father King George III. It was a fashionable era. Women of the landed gentry wore extravagant hats, decorative bonnets, and fancy turbans.

ADULT SUPERVISION REQUIRED

MATERIALS

- ¾-to-1¼-inch-wide sturdy ribbon, such as millinery ribbon wire*
- Scissors
- Needle
- Thread
- 4 safety pins
- Silky scarf with fringe, measuring about 28 by 70 inches
- Saucepan or mixing bowl
- Clothespins, bag clips, or straight pins
- ½-by-1-inch scrap of knit fabric or felt
- Optional: Trims such as fabric or lace ribbon of different widths, second scarf, and feathers

  * If millinery ribbon wire is unavailable, use a similar product such as sturdy cotton twill ribbon, heavy-duty cotton webbing, or belting found at most fabric stores

Turban worn during the Regency period. *Photo by Wendy Reichenthal, courtesy of the Jane Austen Centre in Bath*

THE HATBAND

1. Fit a piece of sturdy ribbon around your head, overlapping about 3 inches. Cut off excess ribbon and stitch the band together where it overlaps. The part you stitched will be the back of the turban.

2. Use two safety pins to mark the front center of the turban and the center back (at the overlap where you just stitched).

3. Fold the scarf in half, bringing the two ends together, and mark the center of the scarf by inserting two safety pins, one at each edge.

4. Hold one scarf safety pin to the safety pin at the back of the headband and then adjust so that the headband is about an inch from the edge of the scarf. Use clothespins to clip the scarf and headband together. Fold the scarf's edge over the back half of the headband, concealing the headband with the scarf. Then

hold this hem in place with clothespins or straight pins.

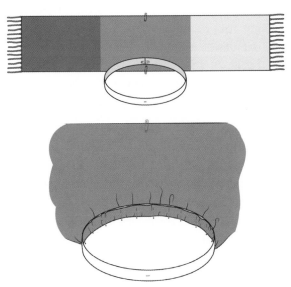

5. Hand-stitch the scarf in place along the entire back half of the headband. Remove all clothespins or straight pins and both safety pins from the back.

6. Mark the middle back of the inside (where the edge of the scarf is visible) of

the turban using a safety pin to attach a scrap of knit fabric or felt.

7. Now bring the other edge of the scarf to the front of the headband, bringing the safety pins together and then adjusting so the headband is about an inch from the scarf's edge. Repeat what you did in step 4, folding the edge of the scarf toward the inside of the turban and securing and sewing this hem along the front half of the headband. Remove all clothespins or straight pins and both safety pins from the front.

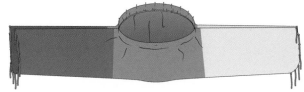

SHAPING THE TURBAN

1. Place the turban over a saucepan or mixing bowl (this will be your mold) so that the outside is facing out and the front is facing you. Gather excess scarf at the crown, or top of the head, and use a clothespin to hold it.

2. Gently twist the right side of the scarf and use a clothespin to hold this twist close to your mold. Then do the same to the left side of the scarf.

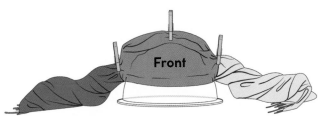

3. Gently twist the entire right side of the scarf. Bring the right end toward the left, going around the front of the turban. Use clothespins to hold the twisted right side of the scarf onto the front of the turban. Continue bringing the right side around, crossing the right end of the scarf over the left end, and lay it in place.

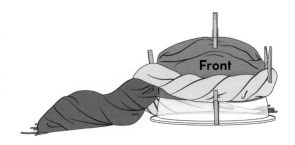

CONTINUED ON NEXT PAGE . . .

4. Gently twist the entire left side of the scarf. Bring the left end up and over the right end as shown.

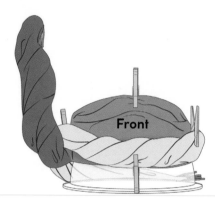

5. Continuing in the same direction you brought the right side (toward the left), bring the left end around to the back of the turban. Use clothespins to hold it onto the back.

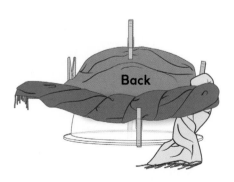

6. Cut the fringe off this left side, close to the scarf but not cutting into the scarf fabric. Fold this edge ½ inch, secure with straight pins, and hand-stitch this hem. This hem does not need to look perfect as it will get tucked into the folds.

7. Continuing in the same direction (toward the left), weave the left end of the scarf through a "hole" created by the first side where it is twisted across the front. Bring the left end of the scarf around the first side and up toward the outside top of the turban. Hide the end of the scarf in a fold here at the top. Use clothespins to hold it in place.

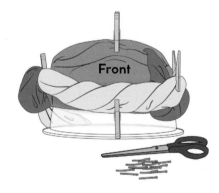

8. Carefully remove the turban from your mold and try it on to see how it fits. Adjust the coils and clothespins as needed to make it fit better.

9. Once the turban size is to your liking, you can stitch it together (see step 10). If you want to make a fancier turban, however, at this point you can weave in a string of beads or fabric ribbon, following the coils of the scarf. If you want a tag to mark the back, stitch the scrap of fabric or felt in place and remove the safety pin.

10. To stitch the turban's coils and embellishments in place, use a needle and thread to tack the coils and embellishments in place all around the headband, removing the clothespins as you work. Try the turban on several times, adding stitches where they are needed. One or two feathers, glued or taped to a safety pin and pinned to the turban, add a nice finishing touch.

Make a Top Hat

During the Regency period, fashionable gentlemen could be seen sporting top hats while strolling through the streets of Bath, attending a ball, or going to the theater.

ADULT SUPERVISION REQUIRED

MATERIALS

- 4 12-by-8-inch sheets of black craft foam, 3 mm thick
- Ruler
- Pencil
- Scissors
- Waxed paper
- Hot-glue gun and glue sticks
- Black electrical tape
- Clothespins

THE FLUE

1. Along the short, 8-inch end of each sheet of craft foam, measure 5 inches and draw a line, making a 5-by-12-inch rectangle on each. Cut out these rectangles to form the flue, or side band, of your top hat.

2. Working on waxed paper to protect your work surface, place the two pieces of foam side-by-side so that the short edge of one is nearly touching the short edge of the other. Place your hot glue gun on your work surface and turn it on. It's ready when glue starts dripping from the nozzle. Working quickly so the glue stays hot, run a bead of hot glue along the entirety of one of these edges. Carefully place the edge of the other sheet of craft foam against this edge, gluing the pieces together along one 5-inch side so that the two pieces are lined up.

3. Cut two 7-inch pieces of black electrical tape. Put one piece along the glued edges, covering the seam you just made, so that there is an inch hanging off either end of foam. Carefully flip over the foam

pieces, and fold these extra inches over to the other side. Now place the second piece of tape over the seam on this side, again folding the extra inches.

4. Fit the long sheet of foam around your head so that the seam you just taped runs vertical and the foam sits on top of your ears. (If you measure below your ears, the finished top hat will be too big. If you measure too far above your ears, the finished top hat will be too small.) Place a clothespin where the sheet overlaps.

5. Place the foam back on your workspace. With a pencil, mark where the clothespin is and then remove the clothespin. Measure how far from the short edge this mark is, and then make a mark the same distance from that short edge, at the other long edge of the foam. With a ruler, draw a straight line parallel to the short edge, connecting these two marks.

Cut the foam with scissors along this line and discard the extra foam.

6. Wrap the piece around your head as before to ensure it fits well atop your ears when the ends are touching. If it's too big, trim the foam as needed. Now use the hot-glue gun to glue the two short edges together, making a cylinder with your foam. Once the glue is dry, add two strips of tape over the seam, like you did in step 3.

THE BRIM

1. Center the flue over a sheet of craft foam. Use a ruler and pencil to draw a circle that is 2 to 3 inches bigger in circumference than the cylinder. Cut this circle out of the foam.

2. Place the cylinder in the center of this large circle. Reach inside the cylinder and trace around the inner edge to mark the hole you will cut in the brim.

3. Gently fold the brim and cut out the center hole.

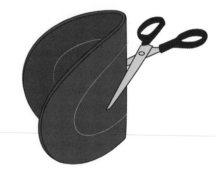

THE CROWN

1. Place the hat upside down on a sheet of foam.

2. Trace a circle around the outside edge of the cylinder. This will be the top, or crown, of the hat.

3. Cut out this circle and place it on your work surface.

CONSTRUCTING YOUR TOP HAT

1. Working quickly so the glue stays hot, run a bead of glue along one edge of the flue.

2. Place the flue onto the brim, lining it up along the brim's hole. Position the edges together all around the circle, pressing gently together as you go. The flue should stay on top of the brim, not inside the hole.

3. Run a bead of glue around the other edge of the flue.

4. Quickly place the hat upside down on top of the circle, attaching the flue to the crown. Position the edges together all around the circle, pressing gently together as you go so the two pieces are attached along the line of glue.

5. To finish the top hat, pick off extra pieces of glue. Add more glue in places as needed to hold it together. You can also cover seams with black electrical tape.

5

LOVE AND FRIENDSHIP

⫷⫸

GROWING UP

Eliza de Feuillide, baby Hastings, and Aunt Philadelphia left for Paris. By the following summer, they returned for a short trip to London on business. It was early July 1789. Jane was 13.

The world was watching Paris. Trouble was brewing there. Angry mobs gathered in the streets. Threats of revolution hung heavy in the heat. The Austens must have had countless questions to ask. Was Eliza's husband joining his regiment to bear "arms against his own countrymen"? What were Louis XVI and his queen, Marie Antoinette, going to do to the revolutionaries?

Shocking news reached London. The English newspaper the *World* reported the events that took place in Paris on July 14, 1789:

The POPULAR PARTY are now completely triumphant. A NATIONAL REVOLUTION, brought about in a period so short, has had no parallel in the History of the World. . . . Three Hundred Thousand Men are in arms. After committing various acts of violence, the Party attacked the Bastile [sic], which they soon broke open; and . . . all the prisoners were set at liberty.

The article continued its description of the "catastrophe." The French revolutionaries burned convents in Paris, beheaded French leaders, and launched a frenzied manhunt for royal family members. They offered a handsome reward to anyone who brought in "the Person of the Queen alive or dead!"

Louis XVI tried to crush the revolution. The people of Paris protested and marched out to Versailles, the monarch's luxurious palace. On October 6, 1789, a crowd gathered like a swarm of angry bees. They demanded Louis XVI, Marie Antoinette, and the royal family leave their château. The mobs took the royals back to Paris, where various leaders of the day attempted to establish democratic rule.

The American Revolution had started the year Jane was born. There were political troubles in India when Uncle Tysoe Hancock and his friend Warren Hastings lived there. Wars and rumors of wars influenced the lives of everyone in Georgian England.

The Austens returned to normal life as well as they could. While they anxiously studied newspapers, talked about terrifying events, and expressed concern about Eliza's husband in France, they were still a long way from Paris.

A LITERARY FAMILY

Jane's brothers were growing up. Her younger brother, Charles, was still at home and receiving his education from their father. Francis, Jane's adventurous brother, finished his training at the

On July 14, 1789, a violent mob of revolutionaries stormed the infamous Bastille prison in Paris, France. *Library of Congress, LC-USZ62-10833*

Royal Naval Academy. At 14, in 1788, he sailed for the East Indies aboard the HMS *Perseverance* as a volunteer. Among his private possessions, he carried a letter written to him by his father. This letter offered spiritual guidance, moral advice, and fatherly affection to the lad. Francis kept this cherished paper with him until he died.

Edward, Jane's fortunate brother, traveled for several years through Europe on a grand tour. Well-to-do young men were sent on these tours to expose them to polished society, current world culture, and famous historic sites. Like an explorer discovering new land in the name of the king, eighteen-year-old Edward hiked the Alps in Switzerland, toured magnificent palaces in Italy, and boated through canals in Amsterdam.

Jane's eldest brother, James, along with her favorite brother, Henry, were both at St. John's College in Oxford. Henry was a student. James had graduated and stayed on as a teacher. These brothers decided to publish a magazine that "offered to the world as a 'rough, but not entirely inaccurate Sketch of the Character, the Manners, and the Amusements of Oxford, at the close of the eighteenth century.'" They called it the *Loiterer*.

Jane continued to write. Romance and friendship were two frequent themes. In Georgian England, popular novels made ridiculous claims about making friends or falling in love. The characters weren't realistic. The plots were outrageous. Jane decided to mock this popular literary trend. She wrote in a literary form known as burlesque, using comedy and silly exaggeration to make fun of popular novels. She also experimented

Edward Austen Knight, Jane's fortunate brother. *Courtesy of the Chawton House Library*

with developing her own witty voice, creating unique characters, and inventing complicated plot twists.

One of the stories she wrote was called "Henry and Eliza." In this story, Jane wrote of the sudden and amazing friendship that formed when Eliza, the heroine, met a wealthy duchess:

Navigate with a Sextant

Two of Jane Austen's brothers were navy men. Both Francis and Charles rose up to become admirals, traveling around the world. They sailed to the Americas and the West Indies, around the Cape of Good Hope, to China, the East Indies, and the Mediterranean Sea.

Navigation skills were important to them, and the sextant, a navigation tool invented in the mid-1700s, was a valuable tool. The sextant measured the altitude of the sun, moon, or stars to help determine the latitude and longitude positions of a ship. It was composed of a 60-degree metal arc with the degrees marked, a telescope, mirrors, and a movable bar. You can make a simple sextant and learn how sailors navigate by measuring the altitude of the moon and stars.

MATERIALS

- Scissors
- 12-inch ruler
- Heavy thread
- Protractor with a small hole in the bottom
- Small weight (metal washer or metal shank button)
- Clear packing tape
- Assistant to help read the sextant

1. Cut a 10-inch length of heavy thread. Tie one end to the small hole in the protractor.

2. Tie the other end of thread to a small weight. This thread and weight are called the *plumb line*.

3. Place the ruler flat on a table in front of you so that the O end is on your left. Put the straight side of the protractor on top of the ruler, about ½-inch from the O end of the ruler, with the curved side of the protractor closest to you. Making sure that the thread hangs freely, tape the protractor's straight edge securely to ruler.

4. On a clear night, go outside and hold the sextant so that the ruler is on top, the protractor is below, and the plumb line hangs straight down. Bring the O end of the ruler close to one eye. Sight along the edge of the ruler to locate the

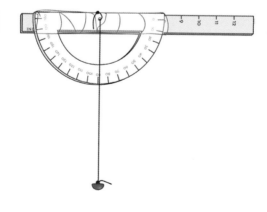

moon or a star. Letting the plumb line hang straight down, ask your assistant to note where the thread falls across the protractor. (Read the inner set of numbers in degrees on the inside arc.) This reading is called the *zenith angle*.

5. Subtract the zenith angle from 90 degrees to find the *altitude angle* of the moon or star. The altitude angle is the height in degrees above the horizon. For example, if your zenith angle is 15 degrees, the altitude angle is 90 – 15 = 75 degrees.

6. To navigate in the northern hemisphere, sailors used a sextant after locating Polaris, the North Star. Since the North Star is directly above the North Pole, calculating its altitude angle told the sailors their *latitude*, the distance north from the equator (measured by degrees). Use your simple sextant to determine your latitude. Use a star chart to help you locate Polaris, measure its zenith angle, then calculate your latitude.

The Dutchess no sooner beheld our Heroine than throwing her arms around her neck, she declared herself so much pleased with her, that she was resolved they never more should part.

Later in the story, readers discover the dark comedy Jane was creating. This same duchess sent out after Eliza "300 armed Men, with orders not to return without their Bodies, dead or alive." This sounded a lot like the newspaper report when the French Revolution began. The *World* newspaper had declared that day, "Three Hundred Thousand Men are in arms," and a reward had been offered for someone to bring back "The Person of the Queen alive or dead!"

Jane moved her own characters from an eternal, exaggerated friendship to an emotional, exaggerated manhunt. She made a grand mockery of popular novels.

In another story, "Jack and Alice," Jane wrote about the friendship that took place when Alice met Lucy:

The perfect form, the beautifull face, & elegant manners of Lucy so won on the affections of Alice that when they parted, which was not till after Supper, She assured her that except her Father, Brother, Uncles, Aunts, Cousins & other relations, Lady Williams, Charles Adams & a few dozen more of particular friends, she loved her better than almost any other person in the world.

What a silly satire this was! First Jane said that Alice and Lucy were best of friends. Then she

showed that Lucy was only Alice's best friend after a long (and funny) line of people.

DAYDREAMS AND DIVERSIONS

It's fun to imagine clever Jane sitting down to write stories as a teenager. Did she chuckle at romantic misadventures she planned for her imaginary characters? Did she daydream about her own future romantic diversions?

In 1789 a new family moved into the neighborhood. A widower named Lovelace Bigg inherited Manydown, a handsome estate near Steventon Parsonage. He and his sons changed their surname to Bigg-Wither. It was a common practice in Georgian England for men (and sometimes women) to change their last name to carry on the name of the family member from whom they inherited their wealth.

Lovelace Bigg-Wither had a large family. Two of his daughters married after moving to Jane's neighborhood. (Their eldest brother had died in 1794, leaving younger brother Harris to inherit his father's great wealth.) Three sisters, who kept the last name Bigg, became Jane and Cassandra's closest friends. Jane and Cassandra spent many happy days visiting Manydown and playing with Elizabeth, Catherine, and Alethea Bigg. Their little brother Harris, more than five years younger than Jane, probably joined in.

It was around this time that Jane got the Steventon marriage register. As rector, her father kept a careful record of all the marriages in the Parish Register of Marriages and Banns. Jane looked over an empty page. There were blanks to fill in. What a delightful game she could play!

First came the Form of an Entry of Publication of Banns. This would be the announcement of her marriage. Who could be her husband? Jane dipped her quill in the bottle of ink and wrote, HENRY FREDERICK HOWARD FITZWILLIAM, OF LONDON. She added her own name as wife, JANE AUSTEN, OF STEVENTON.

Farther down the page were more blanks. This would be for the marriage. Jane wrote the new name of her husband, EDMUND ARTHUR WILLIAM MORTIMER, OF LIVERPOOL? Once again, she added her own name as wife, JANE AUSTEN, OF STEVENTON.

At the bottom of the page, Jane signed the names of two witnesses for the marriage. She wrote, JACK SMITH and JANE SMITH LATE AUSTEN. A third husband indeed. How diverting!

"LOVE AND FREINDSHIP"

On June 13, 1790, Jane finished a new story. She was 14 years old. She called it "Love and Freindship." (There were few regulations in Georgian England regarding spelling, and Jane misspelled *friendship* as she did most words with *ie* in the middle.)

"Love and Freindship" was dedicated to her cousin Eliza. Following the popular novels in Jane's day, it was written as letters. (Stories written as letters between the characters are called epistolary novels.) It was more like a real novel in length and had more developed characters and intricate plots. Completing "Love and Freindship" was a turning point in young Jane's writing.

Like many of her early stories, it was a burlesque, or mockery, of popular novels. Once again Jane made fun of the current literary trends. The plots of many current novels made very little sense, and Jane developed the plot of "Love and Freindship" to be even more disjointed.

Popular novels in Jane's day often had a moral. In "Love and Freindship," Jane showed her characters robbing, lying, and breaking the Ten Commandments without one thought of remorse.

At the time, many fictional characters came from unknown origins, their birth shrouded in mystery. Jane gave her main character such a mysterious past that it took the entire story to explain. Novels were also full of emotional scenes in which ladies fainted or went mad from shocking events. In "Love and Freindship," Jane's characters faint and run mad to a comical extreme. And novels often depicted characters who suffered from amnesia—forgetting things they should have known. Jane's characters forgot even their own relatives.

When her family and friends gathered around the fireside to read aloud to each other, what nights of entertainment Jane's new story provided! Her audience understood every joke Jane made and laughed at all the right places. As Austen juvenilia scholar Juliet McMaster said, "Reading novels and critically reacting to them were clearly the great delights of young Jane Austen's life."

PIANO LESSONS

Years earlier when Jane and Cassandra attended boarding school, both girls probably took piano lessons. For Christmas 1786, after the sisters had returned home for good, the Austens borrowed a pianoforte for Eliza to play. At some point, the Austens bought their own pianoforte. Cassandra lost interest, but not Jane. The liveliness of the melodies brightened her day, and she sat down at the pianoforte nearly every morning and greeted her family with song.

The Austen family owned various music books for playing on the pianoforte. One was a published book with pages of blank music sheets for copying music into by hand. Bound with a soft leather cover, one of the opening pages featured a picture

The pianoforte Jane Austen played looked very similar to the one in this illustration from Jane's novel *Sense and Sensibility*. *"Marianne, wrapped up in her own music," illustrated by Chris Hammond (1860–1900). Wikimedia Commons*

of a cupid. In his hands was a printed banner saying, "Juvenile Songs & Lessons for young beginners who don't know enough to practice."

On page 10 was a song called "Nos Galan." In her own handwriting, Jane copied every note of every song in this book, including "Nos Galan."

> "My loose cash would certainly be employed in improving my collection of music and books."
> *—Sense and Sensibility*

Music from one of Jane's piano books, copied in her own hand. *Courtesy of the Jane Austen's House Museum*

She had borrowed songbooks from other family members and friends to copy into this one. Copying songs into blank music books was part of a young girl's education among the gentry in Georgian England. It wasn't her favorite task to do, but Jane wrote each note neatly.

Jane's piano teacher was George William Chard. He held the prestigious position of assistant organist at Winchester Cathedral, the magnificent church in the county of Hampshire. To earn extra income, he gave piano lessons. Austen scholar and biographer Patrick Piggott noted, "It was the custom then, and for long afterwards, for music teachers to give their lessons at their pupils' homes." Jane had quite an important "music master."

When Mr. Chard arrived at Steventon Parsonage, he listened to Jane's progress. He watched her fingering. He may have sat down and demonstrated the proper way to play. He probably assigned Jane the landmark piano score "The Battle of Prague." Nearly every young lady performed it for family and friends.

Mr. Chard may have also coached Jane in singing. (In later years when he was main organist at Winchester Cathedral, he became choirmaster, training young men to sing.) Jane "had a sweet voice, and sang with feeling." Her music books contained a number of "Scotch and Irish folksongs and ballads."

Mr. Chard had a good ear for music. He also kept a keen ear out for a foxhunt. On days he happened to be in the area during hunting season, locals described what happened if he heard the baying of the foxhounds. "Tally-ho!" Mr. Chard cried. "Go it my Pippins, over hill and dale." Off the music tutor hurried to follow the fox, leaving his piano students behind.

A PREJUDICED HISTORIAN

Jane's brothers loved to hunt. Sometimes when Jane wrote, cozy near the fireplace on a crisp wintry day, her brothers returned from the hunt bringing the fresh air and smell of the outdoors home. From time to time, Jane likely saw James or a neighbor carry home a great rack of antlers from a stag, or male deer, that had been shot.

In February 1791, Jane's eldest brother James shouldered his gun and went stag hunting. On

"Nos Galen"

This winter song was often played on New Year's Eve. Most likely the tune originated in Wales during the 1500s. Dating further back, the merry choruses of "Fa la la la la" probably came from a medieval ballad. Mozart, the famous composer who died in 1791 when Jane was almost 16, used "Nos Galan" as a piano duet with the violin.

In 1784, the piece was published in a book of Welsh songs. Jane may have copied this version into her own book, as this melody has been a favorite for many. New words were eventually written. These lyrics were published in the late 1800s, establishing it as the lively, well-known Christmas carol "Deck the Halls with Boughs of Holly."

> "Every man is surrounded by a neighbourhood of voluntary spies."
> *–Northanger Abbey*

several occasions, the Prince of Wales joined James and his party of hunters. What political gossip may James have shared when he came home?

Strongly opinionated 15-year-old Jane did not like the Prince of Wales. It didn't matter that he was the son of the king, George III. The prince was immoral, extravagant, and vain. She especially did not like that he rented a mansion, Kempshott Park, about five miles from Steventon

(left) **His Royal Highness, George, Prince of Wales.** *Library of Congress, LC-USZ62-107848*

(right) **Images of royal monarchs, illustrated by Cassandra Austen (signed "CE Austen").** *Wikimedia Commons*

Parsonage. His wild parties were a disgrace to their neighborhood.

Jane had definite views about princes, princesses, and monarchs of England. Hitherto, as part of her education, she'd studied the popular four-volume book *The History of England, from the Earliest Times to the Death of George II* by Oliver Goldsmith. Jane didn't just read the pages, however; she also wrote her heated opinions in the margins.

Goldsmith described the Stuarts—Jane's favorite monarchs—as "a family whose misfortunes and misconducts are not to be paralleled in history." What did Jane write in response? She declared with emotion, "A family who were always ill-used, BETRAYED OR NEGLECTED, whose virtues are seldom allowed, while their errors are never forgotten."

Goldsmith included details of a speech by Mr. Walpole, a leading member of the political party known as the Whigs. Jane supported the opposing political party, called the Tories. She wrote a comment about Walpole's speech: "Nobly said! Spoken like a Tory!"

Goldsmith commented that the harshest laws in England were made against "that party that are continually stunning mankind with a cry of freedom." Jane replied, "My Dear Mr. G—, I have lived long enough in the world to know that it is always so."

Finally, a new idea lit up Jane's imagination. She would write her own "History of England"! And she would get Cassandra to help.

Would Cassandra paint a portrait of each monarch Jane included in her book? Cassandra enjoyed the hours she spent with paints and brushes almost as much as Jane did with her pen. The two sisters could entertain each other with their project. After revising it to her liking, Jane copied it by hand into her notebook *Volume the Second*.

A satire, or mockery, of Oliver Goldsmith's *History of England*, Jane's "History of England" included a comic report of each monarch from Henry IV to Charles I. Cassandra painted a portrait of each one. For monarchs Jane liked, Cassandra's art portrays tender poses. Mary, Queen of Scots, was Jane's favorite, as can be seen by the pretty picture Cassandra painted (on the bottom left). But fye! Oh! fye! Jane declared Elizabeth I was a "disgrace to humanity, that pest of society." How Jane must have laughed to see Cassandra's illustration (on the bottom right). Pompous feathers sprouting from her head, an oversized hooked nose, and a scowling face combined for a portrait in which Jane surely took delight.

Finally, the project was done. Jane dated the pages *Saturday, Nov: 26th, 1791.*

GROWING UP

How 16-year-old Jane loved to dance! Tonight she was getting ready to attend a ball, one of her first. A public ball was being held at the Hampshire Club in nearby Basingstoke. Would her friends the Bigg sisters be there with their younger brother Harris? It was October 4, 1792. Both she and Cassandra were going.

Alas! can you help me with my buttons?

How does my hair look?

May I borrow a pair of your gloves—one of mine has a hole!

Pray tell! who do you think we shall dance with?

It's fun to imagine conversations between Jane and Cassandra as they got ready. How diverting!

Lady's dressing table. *Photo by author, courtesy of the Trustees of Stoneleigh Abbey*

Say It with Satire

I dare say Jane Austen loved a satire. What is a satire? It's usually a humorous look at the wrongs of the world and can be a clever way to share your opinion with others. Jane held strong views about the politics of England, so she chose to write one of her most opinionated satires, "The History of England," about this topic. In satire, writers often employ certain writing techniques to underscore their opinions humorously:

Irony is saying one thing but meaning the opposite. For example, you have a new puppy and you discover the puppy ate your homework. You could say, using irony, "I'm so happy to know our puppy is well fed." Irony helps capture the attention of your audience and make them interested in your topic.

Sarcasm is using irony but with a "bite." For example, there might be a lot of new houses going up in your city but no new highways, causing serious traffic jams. It used to only take 20 minutes to get to school, and now it takes an hour. You could say, "Wasn't our city council thoughtful? They gave us lots of time to make new friends each morning on the way to school." The statement uses irony in a way meant to wound, or insult, the city council. Sarcasm is often used in a satire to prove an important point.

Hyperbole is the use of extreme exaggeration. For example, if you want to encourage people to help rescue cats at the animal shelter, you could say, "I was thinking of adopting 500 kittens myself, but thought other people might want a pet too." In a satire, hyperboles are used to add humor or to bring a strong reaction from the reader concerning your topic.

Understating is treating something really important as if it is extremely unimportant. For example, you might be worried the city is putting a landfill near your house. You could say, "There's a new landfill in our neighborhood. I'm buying a pine-scented air freshener to hang in my room." Such a small reaction to a comparably big problem makes the new landfill sound less important than it really is. Understating is used to bring a laugh from your reader or to encourage your reader to think twice about the point you are trying to make.

Persuasion is providing convincing reasons that your stance on a topic is the best stance to take. For example, if you want to convince people that establishing a colony on Mars is the best option for mankind, you could say, "Life will be better on Mars. You'll live in the best neighborhood on the planet!" In a satire, persuasion helps bring your readers into agreement with your opinion.

MATERIALS

- Computer with internet access
- Notebook and pen or pencil or computer with word-processing software

1. Read "The History of England," available at the website *Jane Austen for Kids* (www.nancy isanders.com/jane-austen). First read the essay straight through to get the overall feel. Then read each section slowly. Identify parts in which Jane used irony, sarcasm, or other writing techniques to create her satire.

2. Make a notebook of topics you have strong opinions about. What do you see going on around you that you'd like to change?

3. Pick one of the topics and list opinions you have about it. Ask others to give you their opinions and write these in your notebook. Look at blogs, websites, articles, or books about the topic and note any other helpful information you find.

4. Outline your satire by looking at your notes and deciding in what order you want to discuss each important point. Which of the writing techniques mentioned earlier can you use to make your argument?

5. Write your satire, following the organization you just outlined and using the techniques you chose. Remember to be persuasive. You can make your essay serious or you can add humor (as Jane Austen liked to do) to make it fun.

"A lady's imagination is very rapid; it jumps from admiration to love, from love to matrimony in a moment." *–Pride and Prejudice*

Jane and her sister were growing up, and Cassandra had fallen in love. Rev. Thomas Fowle, one of Mr. Austen's pupils, captured Cassandra's affections. Earlier, Cousin Eliza had written to Cousin Phylly, "As to the young Ladies I hear they are perfect Beauties and of course gain 'hearts by the dozens.'" In another letter, she declared, "I hear [Cassandra & Jane] are two of the prettiest Girls in England."

In a letter to Phylly written the same month as the ball, Eliza added, "Cassandra & Jane are both very much grown (The latter is now taller than myself) and greatly improved as well in Manners as in Person both of which are now much more formed than when You saw them. They are I think equally sensible, and both so to a degree seldom met with, but still My Heart gives the preference to Jane, whose kind partiality to me, indeed requires a return of the same nature."

Their youngest brother, Charles, left home to attend the Royal Naval Academy in Portsmouth. Francis was on his way to becoming a lieutenant while still in the East Indies. Henry was at Oxford, having just graduated. Their two older brothers, James and Edward, were married. On December 11, 1792, just five days before Jane's 17th birthday, their cousin Jane Cooper got married too.

Statue of Jane Austen. *Photo by Jeff Sanders, courtesy of the Jane Austen Centre in Bath*

Dance the Boulanger

> "We were at a Ball on Saturday I assure you. We dined at Goodnestone & in the Evening danced two Country Dances and the Boulangeries."
> —Jane Austen, in a letter to Cassandra

The Boulanger (or Boulangeries) was often the last dance. A simple circular dance, it was a fun way to end the ball. Not only did Jane dance it, she had her characters in *Pride and Prejudice* dance it too.

Here are the steps to the Boulanger.

Four couples stand facing each other, with men on the left side of their partners.

Start the music.

A1

All dancers hold hands, forming a circle. With a skipping step, circle left for eight steps.

A2

With a skipping step, circle right for eight steps.

B

Man 1 (M1) takes Woman 1's (W1) right hand with his right hand. Couple 1 (C1) twirls once around while holding hands. W1 stays in the middle of the circle.

M1 takes W2 by the left hand with his left hand and they twirl once around. W2 returns to her original place in the circle.

M1 returns to the middle and turns W1 by the right hand as before.

M1 turns W3 by the left hand.

M1 returns to the middle and turns W1 by the right hand.

M1 turns W4 by the left hand.

M1 returns to the middle and turns partner by the right hand, then they return to their original positions.

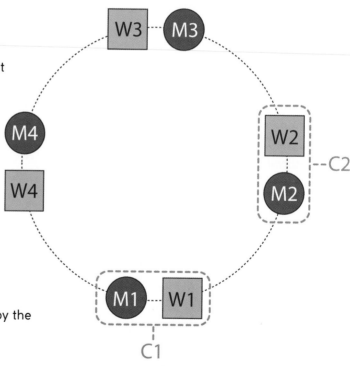

A1

All dancers hold hands, forming a circle. With a skipping step, circle left for eight steps.

A2

With a skipping step, circle right for eight steps.

B

M2 takes W2's right hand with his right hand. C2 twirls once around while holding hands. W2 stays in the middle of the circle.

M2 turns W3 by the left hand.

M2 returns to the middle and turns W2 by the right hand.

M2 turns W4 by the left hand.

M2 returns to the middle and turns W2 by the right hand.

M2 turns W1 by the left hand.

M2 returns to the middle and turns partner by the right hand, then they return to their original positions.

Repeat these steps until each couple takes their turn to move around the circle and return to their original positions.

Dance scene. *Photo by author, courtesy of the Jane Austen Centre in Bath*

Many weddings (and funerals) took place inside St. Nicholas Church, Steventon. Jane attended St. Nicholas for 25 years. Her father was rector here.
Photo by author, courtesy of St. Nicholas Church by kind permission of Steventon PCC

ceremony. He and Cassandra planned to marry as soon as he could afford it. Captain and Mrs. Williams signed their names to the Parish Register of Marriages and Banns. Rev. Tom Fowle signed his name as the clerk.

Witnesses were needed. Edward Cooper, Jane Cooper's older brother, signed first. Cassandra then stepped forward. Finally, it was Jane's turn. Jane signed on the very last line. This time, it was official.

THE REIGN OF TERROR

News of war hung over Jane's family. Everywhere she went people talked about it. France was in the middle of a revolution that would last 10 years.

Cousin Eliza was distressed. Her husband, the Comte de Feuillide, had visited England during Aunt Philadelphia's final days and death but had been called urgently back to Paris. Now he was in the center of the war zone, where political revolutionaries sentenced masses of French aristocrats to the guillotine, a large device used to behead the condemned. His life was in danger.

Eliza stayed most of the winter with Jane and her family. Eliza scanned the newspapers for news from Paris. The danger. The threats. The terror. What would happen to France? What would happen to the comte? On January 21, 1793, King Louis XVI of France was sent to the guillotine.

It must have been difficult for life to go on in the face of such upheaval abroad. Two days after the French king's execution, however, Jane's fortunate brother Edward Austen Knight and his wife,

And now, a number of weeks after the local ball Jane had attended, Steventon Parsonage was filled to overflowing. Cousin Eliza and her son, Hastings, were staying with the Austens. They had come to visit after Eliza's mother, Aunt Philadelphia, had passed away. Cousin Jane Cooper was there too. She had come to visit after her father's recent death.

Hitherto, a shadow of mourning hung over Steventon Parsonage. Today, however, promised to be happier. Today was a wedding day!

The events of the day were joyful and romantic. Pretty Jane Cooper stood next to her dashing new husband, Captain Thomas Williams of the British Royal Navy. Tom Fowle performed the

Elizabeth, had their first child, a girl they named Fanny. Jane became Aunt Jane for the first time and wrote a short piece dedicated to her niece.

At 17, Jane now had a collection of manuscripts. By this time, she was writing longer stories. Her new works, such as "Lesley Castle," "Evelyn," and "Catherine," were more serious and thoughtful. They were still humorous—how Jane loved to laugh!—but her characters had more depth and her plots were more involved.

In March 1793 Jane and all England heard the news: the French Revolution had entered its darkest days. It became known as the Reign of Terror. People whispered of the horrors of the guillotine.

On April 15, 1793, Jane's eldest brother James Austen and his wife had their first daughter, Jane "Anna" Austen. Aunt Jane wrote another piece and dedicated it to her new niece.

By now, Jane's three writing notebooks were almost full. *Volume the First*, *Volume the Second*, and *Volume the Third* contained nearly 30 stories in her neat handwriting. She wrote one final piece, a poem she called "Ode to Pity." It was a satire on sentimental poetry popular in that day and is considered the last piece of juvenilia Jane wrote.

In August, threats of invasion spread like wildfire through the English countryside. The revolution in France was heading for England! Ten thousand British troops marched into Brighton, a seaside town in southeast England. They would provide a line of defense along the seashore against any French warships that tried to attack.

Jane started writing a new story called *Lady Susan*. Even though the story is a comedy, the main character is probably the darkest heroine Jane ever created. Perhaps she was reacting to the frightening environment around her.

With so many soldiers stationed on the coast and nothing to do but wait, card games and dancing helped pass the time. Scholars think Jane visited the coastal city of Southampton to attend a ball that December. Soldiers in their bright-red coats were stationed there as well.

That winter, the news that Jane and all her family had been dreading from Paris suddenly arrived. On February 22, 1794, Eliza's husband was sent to the guillotine.

Jane was 18. Pray tell, what would happen now?

A 3,000-year-old obelisk from Egypt marks the site where the guillotine once stood in Paris, France.
Library of Congress, LC-USZ62-1232

Sew a Reticule

Ladies in Georgian England carried a reticule, an elegant drawstring purse. It was just big enough to hold a few small personal items.

MATERIALS

- Tissue paper
- Tape measure or small ruler
- ⅓ yard of stiff, nonstretchy fabric such as silk, lace, velvet, or a slightly stiff polyester
- Straight pins
- Scissors
- Chalk
- Lace, doily, ribbon, tassel, or beads
- Sewing needle
- Thread matching fabric color
- Fabric glue (optional)
- Thimble (optional)
- 2 yards ¼-inch-wide fabric ribbon
- Safety pin

  (Option: Instead of sewing, reticule may be assembled using fabric glue or iron-on hem tape with adult supervision.)

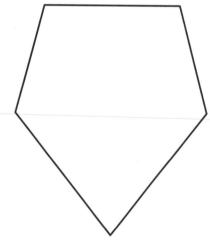

1. Use the shape provided here as a guide for drawing your pattern. Draw the shape on tissue paper. It can be any size. This will be your pattern. Make the pattern a little larger than the finished reticule, allowing for ½-inch seams along the edges and a 2-inch top casing for the drawstrings. For a reticule that measures 8-by-12-inches, draw a pattern that is about 9-by-14-inches.

2. Place two pieces of fabric on top of each other, and pin your pattern to them. Cut through the fabric around the pattern and remove the pins. These two pieces of fabric will be the front and back of your purse.

3. With chalk, trace along the right or left edge of each piece of fabric on one side, about a half inch from the edge. This ½ inch is your seam allowance. Draw two more lines along the top edge of each piece of fabric, one 1 inch from the top edge and another 2 inches from the top edge. The side of fabric with the chalk is the "wrong" side of the fabric, which will be on the inside of the bag.

4. Decorate the other side (or the "right" side of the fabric) of one of the pieces with embellishments such as a doily, ribbon, lace, or fringe, stitching or gluing the embellishment in place. This will be the front piece of your bag. Be sure to keep the embellishment at least an inch from the edge of the fabric.

5. To add a tassel to the bottom front, stitch the tassel's top loop in place on the seam allowance so the stitching will not show on the finished reticule. Pin the tassel in place or tack it with several large, loose stitches (that you will remove later) so it won't slip around.

6. Flip the front piece over so that the right side (with the embellishments) is facedown and the wrong side is faceup. Fold the top edge down to the 1-inch mark, and one more time to the 2-inch mark. Pin this fold in place. This forms

the casing where the drawstring will go. Stitch along the bottom of the fold, leaving the sides of the fold open. Remove the pins.

7. Repeat step 6 on the other piece of fabric.

8. Pin front to the back, right sides together as shown.

9. Stitch the sides together along the ½-inch seam, leaving the top open. Do not stitch the sides of the casing; leave them open for the drawstrings. When you stitch around the bottom point, be careful that you only catch the top loop of the tassel in the seam. Add a second row of stitching on top of the first at the bottom point for extra sturdiness.

10. Turn the reticule right-side out.

11. For drawstrings, cut two 1-yard pieces of ¼-inch-wide ribbon. Attach a safety pin to one end of one piece of ribbon and insert this end into the casing opening on the right side of the front. Thread this through the casing and pull it out of the opening on the left side of the front.

Thread this through the nearest opening on the back until it comes out the back casing on the same side you inserted it. Center the ribbon and remove the safety pin.

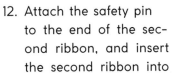

12. Attach the safety pin to the end of the second ribbon, and insert the second ribbon into the casing opening on the left side of the front. Thread this through the casing and pull it out of the opening on the right side of the front. Thread this through the nearest opening on the back until it comes out the back casing on the same side you started. Center the ribbon and remove the safety pin.

13. Determine how long you want your drawstrings. Cut the ribbons to this length. On each side of the reticule, tie the ribbon ends together in an overhand knot.

PERSUASION

--≪≪◆≫≫--

LITERARY MASTERPIECES

On Jane's 19th birthday, December 16, 1794, she received a special gift from her parents: a small writing desk. She could set it on top of a table and write on it. It was the perfect size for holding her papers.

What would Jane write now? She had finished adding stories to her three notebooks. She didn't want to write childish stories like those anymore. She was a young woman now. She had experienced too many life events to think or feel like a child. She had lived during the American Revolution and nearly died when

Jane Austen at her writing desk. *Photo by author, courtesy of the Jane Austen Centre in Bath*

> "To be fond of dancing was a certain step towards falling in love."
>
> *—Pride and Prejudice*

British troops returned home with a deadly disease. Now the French Revolution had seized Jane's family in its grip.

Tragedies weren't the only events Jane had experienced. Her brother Edward had become heir to grand estates. Two brothers had married, as had her cousin. Her sister was engaged. Now she was an aunt twice over. These were happy events.

Perhaps thinking of her own life and the way historical events had overlapped with the personal joys and sorrows her family experienced, Jane decided to write about daily life among the English gentry. It's very likely that she wanted to show the parts of life that happened in England that never made it into the history books.

She also decided to only write about what she knew. Some novelists, then as now, wrote about things they never personally experienced. Her stories wouldn't be like those. Her invented characters would be so believable everyone would think real people had inspired them. Her imaginary plots would seem true.

ELINOR AND MARIANNE

Jane and Cassandra shared a bedroom all their lives. Every day when Jane ate dinner, Cassandra was at the table too. Every evening when Jane listened to their father read aloud, Cassandra listened too.

Jane had an idea for a story. True to her particular philosophy, it would be about a topic she knew: the relationship between two sisters. She would draw material from her own life to write her first full-length novel.

On crisp fall days, Jane and Cassandra walked together over the fields to visit their neighbors. The Digweeds lived closest to them, in the house next to St. Nicholas Church. The Biggs and Bigg-Withers lived a little farther away at Manydown House.

The two sisters walked through piles of red, yellow, and brown autumn leaves crunching beneath their feet. Jane probably shared her ideas out loud. Jane planned to feature two sisters in her story, along with a third sister and other family members. The eldest sister, Elinor, would be wise and represent common sense. The next-younger sister, Marianne, would be passionate and represent sensibility. What did Cassandra think? It's easy to imagine them discussing Jane's new characters as they walked.

On warm spring days when the lanes were filled with puddles, Jane and Cassandra strapped pattens onto their feet. Pattens were a curious invention. A sort of high-heeled wooden clog, pattens helped keep their feet out of the mud. Clinking and clunking their way through the slush, their walking was clumsy.

By the time the two sisters returned home from visiting, they were ready to relax. Jane wrote her ideas on fresh sheets of paper, then read these sections aloud to the family.

Jane's days of writing silly nonsense were behind her. Though she still wrote humor, now she wrote from her heart. *Elinor and Marianne* was a story about falling in love—with the wrong people and hopefully the right.

AN EXCEEDING GOOD BALL

The Christmas season of 1795 brought countless diversions. Jane attended not one, not two, not even three balls. Nay, a series of four deliciously delightful balls were held in her neighborhood that holiday, and Jane attended them all. With special interest, too, for Jane had met a new friend. Thomas Lefroy was visiting his aunt and uncle's home at Ashe Rectory. Jane and Tom met at the first ball and became fast friends.

On Friday, January 8, 1796, Jane dressed for the evening. This was the third ball that Christmas. It may have taken several hours just to curl and "dress" her hair. Sometimes Jane might enlist Cassandra to help. This holiday season, though, Cassandra was unavailable. She was visiting her future in-laws while her fiancé, the reverend, was at sea as chaplain to a friend's military regiment. Sometimes Jane paid a professional to style her hair. For other events, she had help from a local villager such as Nanny Littlewart.

Ready for the ball, Jane buttoned on her pelisse, a long coat. She stepped outside the parsonage. It would be a short carriage drive with her family to Manydown, the mansion where Elizabeth, Catherine, and Alethea Bigg lived with their brother

A pelisse coat owned by Jane Austen. *Reproduced by kind permission courtesy of Hampshire Cultural Trust*

Curl Your Hair

At 22 years old, Jane wrote to Cassandra just after a haircut, "I have made myself two or three caps to wear of evenings since I came home, and they save me a world of torment as to hair-dressing, which at present gives me no trouble beyond washing and brushing, for my long hair is always plaited [braided] up out of sight, and my short hair curls well enough to want no papering. I have had it cut lately by Mr. Butler."

In Georgian England, a sister or maid usually helped young ladies curl their hair. When Jane wanted curls, she had her hair rolled up in strips of paper. This process was called papering. When she untied the strips, she would have a head full of ringlets. Jane preferred wearing a cap and letting a few curls peek out around her face. One evening she was persuaded to wear a velvet sash around her head and let her curls hang down her back.

Follow these steps to curl your hair like Jane might have done. This activity works best with medium-length or long hair.

MATERIALS

- Fabric, such as an old T-shirt (or paper towels)
- Scissors
- Brush and comb
- Spray bottle of water
- Assistant

1. Use scissors to cut fabric into 2-by-12-inch strips. T-shirt or soft knit fabric is easiest to work with. (If using paper towels, fold each one into a strip.)

2. Brush your hair until it is smooth and manageable and dampen it slightly with water.

3. Gather a small section of hair in your hand. Smaller bunches make tighter curls, and thicker bunches make looser curls. Place the ends of these strands of hair in the center of a fabric strip.

4. Wrap the strip one time around the end of the hair strands.

5. Roll the hair up until you reach the crown of your head. Gently tie the strip into a loose overhand knot. Repeat this process, asking your assistant to help, for as many curls as you want to have.

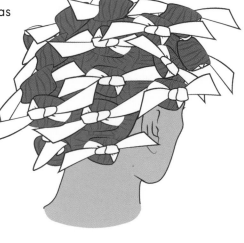

6. Allow your hair to dry for a at least an hour, or sleep in the strips overnight. When ready, untie the knots and unfurl your hair. Gently shake out the curls. Style it or brush it to achieve the look you like best.

Wear Regency-Style Side Whiskers

Charles Austen, Jane's youngest brother, posed in his striking British naval uniform when his portrait was painted. His side whiskers slanted toward his mouth in a popular style seen in many portraits from the Regency era.

According to Miss Lisa Brown's Guide to Dressing for a Regency Ball, "The general rule was that 'side whiskers' were to extend no lower than a line connecting the bottom of the ear lob[e] and the corner of the mouth. . . . Take a yard of string, grasp center in mouth, run ends behind the ears and then up to meet on top of head. Tie a bow, shave anything below the string (and remove string!)."

Use string to measure and makeup to fill in your side whiskers so you can step out Regency style.

MATERIALS

- 3-foot length of string
- Makeup brushes, including a blush brush and a smaller eye shadow brush
- Eye shadow in browns or blacks (or to match your hair color)
- Mascara with a bristle brush, brown or black (or to match your hair color)

Charles Austen, sporting his Regency-style side whiskers.
Photo by author, courtesy of the Jane Austen Centre in Bath

1. Hold the middle of a piece of string in your mouth. To measure the length of your side whiskers, bring each end of the string below your ear, then up to the crown of your head. Tie the string in a bow at the top.

2. With the string in place, use makeup brushes to apply eye shadow as a base for your side whiskers above the string. Follow the style shown in the portrait of Charles Austen, sweeping down from your side whiskers toward your mouth. Use a smaller makeup brush to end the base with a point toward your mouth.

3. After the basic shape is filled in, remove the string. Apply several layers of eye shadow until your side whiskers are as dark as you'd like the base to be.

4. Brush mascara over the area you covered with eye shadow. Use an upward motion to catch the mascara in your facial hair, no matter how fine it is. You will be surprised at how real your side whiskers look!

Harris Bigg-Wither. Jane's dearest friends were hosting tonight's ball.

Arriving at their destination, Jane stepped into the elegant surroundings of Manydown. Lively music invited the young folks to choose partners. Most likely a group of hired musicians played violins at one end of a great room while a long row of couples twirled through each selection they played.

Jane and her new friend Tom found each other in the crowded room. How Jane's eyes must have shone as Tom took her hand and passed her round through the steps of the country-dances. Jane flattered herself for demonstrating particular attention to Tom as her favorite dancing partner, unlike friends of hers who danced with random partners throughout the evening.

As the night wore on, the dancers built up a keen appetite. Smells of a delicious spread invited them into the greenhouse. Candlelight lit up Jane's magical night as if a thousand stars were shining.

"The greenhouse was illuminated in a very elegant manner," Jane later wrote in a letter to her sister. "I am almost afraid to tell you how my Irish friend [Tom Lefroy] and I behaved. Imagine to yourself everything most profligate and shocking in the way of dancing and sitting down together."

The following Friday was to be the fourth and final neighborhood ball of the year. Jane wrote to Cassandra, "I look forward with great impatience to it, as I rather expect to receive an offer from my friend in the course of the evening. I shall refuse him, however, unless he promises to give away his white coat." Jane also confided in that letter,

Thomas Langlois Lefroy (1776-1869)

With five older sisters to think of, Tom Lefroy grew up under high expectations. His family planned his future even when he was still a lad. Tom's wealthy great-uncle, Benjamin Langlois, guided Tom's education and promised to provide financially for him if he succeeded in school and married well.

Around Tom's 20th birthday, he took a much-needed break from his studies and visited Aunt and Uncle Lefroy (Steventon Parsonage's neighbors). Over Christmas, Tom attended a series of neighborhood balls, where he met and danced with budding writer Jane Austen. When the holiday season ended, Tom returned to London. He became a lawyer and married Mary Paul, sister of his schoolmate. They settled in Ireland. Within a year, Mary's brother died, and she inherited substantial wealth. With his successful law practice, Tom became a member of Parliament as well as the Lord Chief Justice of Ireland. In his 90s, when Jane Austen's fame was established, Tom was asked about her. He shared that he once felt a "boyish love" for her.

Tom Lefroy. *Photo by author, courtesy of the Jane Austen Centre in Bath*

"I mean to confine myself in future to Mr. Tom Lefroy, for whom I do not care sixpence."

Because of her characteristic wit, it's hard to tell how serious Jane was in these letters—sharing how she expected to receive a marriage proposal yet joking that she would say no unless he wore a fashionable outfit. And then the winking irony of her confession that she would "confine" herself to Tom yet didn't care for him—was Jane falling in love?

The morning of Friday, January 15, arrived. It was the day of the ball. Jane jotted one more quick note to Cassandra. By this time, however, something had changed. In a very different tone, Jane wrote, "At length the day is come on which I am to flirt my last with Tom Lefroy, and when you receive this it will be over. My tears flow as I write at the melancholy idea. . . . There is a report that Tom is going to be married to a Lichfield lass."

What had happened? Unfortunately, the mystery remains unsolved, even after 200 years; no other letters are known to exist that provide evidence for the truth. Many of Jane's letters from January 15 until August 23, 1796, were lost—destroyed by Cassandra or others. No letters remain from that silent period to help so many "greedy detectives,"

> "You pierce my soul. I am half agony, half hope. . . . I have loved none but you."
> —*Persuasion*

as Joan Austen-Leigh, one of James's descendants, affectionately labeled Janeites.

In the absence of letters, scholars have examined various clues to try to piece together the events. One suggestion is that the Lefroy family expected Tom, as the eldest son in his large family, to marry a woman of fortune. He would have been able to provide for his sisters and mother if this happened. Some think that when Tom's relatives realized he was falling in love with Jane, they whisked him away and sent him back to school. Jane, even though she was one of the landed gentry, came from a family without fortune. She had no dowry, no inheritance to bring to her wedding.

A WHIRL OF WORDS

Growing up in Georgian England, Jane knew many families among the gentry expected their oldest sons to marry well. A family's eldest son inherited an ancient estate, which was expensive to maintain. He needed a wife with a large fortune to keep up the estate and pass it on to the next generation.

Yet witty, wise, tenderhearted Jane also understood the value of marrying for love.

After Tom Lefroy came into her life and left, Jane picked up her pen and wrote with passion. She wrote about young men and women in Georgian England who were persuaded to marry (or not) for financial reasons. She wrote about others who refused to marry for any reason except love. Jane wrote about poignant complexities of the human heart because she was writing from her own.

Still working on *Elinor and Marianne*, she started writing a new novel called *First Impressions*. In 1797, after about one year, she finished the initial draft. The following year she finished the draft of *Elinor and Marianne* and renamed it *Sense and Sensibility*. Jane then began working on a third novel called *Susan*.

The last four years had been emotional ones for Jane and her family. It's amazing she wrote three novels in such a short time, but it's even more astounding when we understand all that had happened.

In April 1797, Cassandra's fiancé, Tom Fowle, died of yellow fever while in Santo Domingo. In December of that year, Jane's favorite brother,

The post office, London, 1809.
Library of Congress, LC-USZ62-98220

Sense and Sensibility by Jane Austen

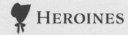 ## HEROINES

Elinor Dashwood
Marianne Dashwood

HEROES

Edward Ferrars
Colonel Brandon

 ## HOUSES

Norland Park: Large estate of the Dashwood family before their father died
Barton Cottage: Small home the Dashwood family moves to after their father's death

OPENING LINE

"The family of Dashwood had long been settled in Sussex."

FAMOUS QUOTE

"The more I know of the world, the more am I convinced that I shall never see a man whom I can really love. I require so much!"

 ## SUMMARY

When their father unexpectedly dies, three sisters and their mother are left practically penniless because of the laws of inheritance. Their half-brother and his selfish wife inherit it all. Elinor, the eldest sister, represents sense and copes with their situation in a practical way. Marianne, representing sensibility and passion, deals with everything in an emotional and dramatic way. Forced out of their grand estate at Norland Park, they move into humble Barton Cottage, neighbors now to Colonel Brandon. Elinor falls in love with Edward Ferrars, and Marianne is rescued by her Willoughby. But as an eldest son, will Edward be disinherited if he marries a woman with no dowry? And can poor, dependent Willoughby afford to marry only for love? With unexpected plot twists along with honorable and dishonorable intentions, each character chooses his or her own fate in the end.

Henry, married Cousin Eliza, as it was a common practice in those days for cousins to marry. Finally, in 1798, Jane's fortunate brother Edward inherited the magnificent estates he'd been promised by the Knight relatives.

Sometimes Jane spent weeks visiting friends or family. Sometimes it was Cassandra who was gone. Whenever Jane and Cassandra were separated, letters flew between them. These letters give us a glimpse of the happy days and hard times Jane experienced while she was busy creating her masterpieces.

From Steventon Parsonage, Jane walked down to the Deane Gate Inn and left her letters. Coaches brought Cassandra's letters there for Jane to pick up. In this way, the two sisters remained close even when they were apart.

MR. AUSTEN'S DECISION

One November evening in 1797, 21-year-old Jane sat with her family, reading aloud to them a section of her three-volume novel *First Impressions*. Eventually she would rename it *Pride and Prejudice*. The group around the fireside was smaller than in years past. Mr. Austen no longer tutored pupils. He was slowing down in his older years. It was just Jane, Cassandra, and their parents at home now.

An idea had been growing in Mr. Austen's mind. As he listened to Jane's story, he recognized his daughter's genius. He was persuaded that her book was just as good, if not better, than the published novels in his bookcases. He made a decision. He would try to get one of Jane's novels published.

Pride and Prejudice silk wall hanging by world-renowned textile artist **Linda Straw.** *Photo by author, courtesy of the Jane Austen Centre in Bath*

Mr. Austen wrote to a London publisher, "I have in my possession a manuscript novel, comprising 3 vols., about the length of Miss Burney's *Evelina*. . . . Should you give any encouragement, I will send you the work." He folded up his letter, addressed it to Messrs. Cadell, and sent it on its way.

Jane didn't have to wait long for the response. They quickly replied by post. Messrs. Cadell were not interested. Fye! They would not even look at it.

It was Jane's first rejection, but it would not stop her. She continued to write.

THE STORM

In May 1799 Jane's fortunate brother Edward Austen Knight arrived at Steventon Parsonage with his wife, Elizabeth, and two of their children. They were on their way to the city of Bath. Edward, feeling vaguely ill, sought the doctors and healing

What Jane Austen Read

Jane loved to read! From Shakespeare to Sir Walter Scott, she read a variety of books. James Edward Austen-Leigh explained, "Amongst her favorite writers, Johnson in prose, Crabbe in verse, and Cowper in both, stood high." Her biographer Claire Tomalin added that Jane also had favorite women authors, "among them Charlotte Lennox, Fanny Burney, Charlotte Smith, Maria Edgeworth, [and] Hannah Cowley."

FANNY BURNEY (1752–1840)

Shy and quiet, Fanny Burney surprised England's fashionable circles with her literary gem *Evelina, or The History of a Young Lady's Entrance into the World*. Published in 1778, it was a novel about proper manners and improper blunders in London. She followed this novel with others, including *Cecilia* (not quite as well received) and *Camilla* (a blockbuster). Though her work was first published anonymously, Burney's identity soon was revealed, and she became famous. She moved in great literary circles that included Samuel Johnson, a friend of her father's. Jane read Burney's novels and knew Burney's characters well. Many Austen scholars feel Jane's own novels were influenced by Burney's works. Burney's novels also helped set the stage for Jane to write about similar topics.

MARIA EDGEWORTH (1767–1849)

Famous for her nonfiction, children's stories, and novels about Ireland, Maria Edgeworth's works affected such budding authors as Jane Austen and Sir Walter Scott. Her characters and their use of dialogue were among her greatest achievements. Jane Austen enjoyed Edgeworth's *Belinda*, a novel about manners, class, and society. In a letter to her young niece and aspiring novelist Anna Austen, Jane wrote, "I have made up my mind to like no Novels really, but Miss Edgeworth's, Yours & my own." High praise indeed, even if written in jest. When Jane's novel *Emma* was published, Jane asked her publisher to send a complimentary copy to Maria Edgeworth.

SAMUEL JOHNSON (1709–1784)

Known for his witty sayings and many published works, Samuel Johnson greatly influenced English literature. In 1755 he published a monumental two-volume *Dictionary of the English Language*, which launched him into fame. Along with political essays and a number of other works, he also wrote a landmark eight-volume edition on Shakespeare and a number of volumes on English poets. Jane was eager to read his biography in 1791, a few years after his death. In a letter to Cassandra, she spoke of him as "my dear Dr. Johnson." She felt he had no equal.

SIR WALTER SCOTT (1771–1832)

A popular author in Jane's day, Scott was well known for poems such as *Marmion* and *The Lady of the Lake*. Later, he became famous for historical novels, including *Rob Roy* and *Ivanhoe*, often set during the days of knights and damsels. Jane enjoyed Scott's poetry. He wrote only three novels before she died, so she never saw Scott's later works. Those of his novels she read, however, she admired. Jane was also aware that Scott read some of her novels. She *didn't* know that he wrote in his diary, "That young lady had a talent for describing the involvements and feelings and characters of ordinary life, which is to me the most wonderful I ever met with."

waters for which that city was known. Would Jane and Mother Austen want to join them?

At 23 years old, Jane was always ready for adventure, even if it meant going to Bath, a city she was not fond of. The party stopped midway on their journey in the town of Devizes. She wrote to Cassandra, "At Devizes we had comfortable rooms and a good dinner, to which we sat down about five; amongst other things we had asparagus and a lobster, which made me wish for you, and some cheesecakes."

Umbrellas greeted them like a flock of bothersome crows the next day as their carriage rolled into Bath. It was raining, dismally gloomy, and dirty—as usual. Alas! how Jane disliked Bath.

They stopped at No. 1 Paragon Buildings to check on their aunt and uncle. James and Jane Leigh Perrot were related to Jane on her mother's side. James was Mrs. Austen's brother.

The muddy puddles swirled too deeply for Jane and the others to step out. The door to their uncle's home opened. Frank, their uncle's servant, rushed out. He stood in the rain just long enough to apologize. Uncle James felt too ill to come out in this weather. With promises of visits on sunnier days, their carriage rolled onward.

Bath was hot and dirty. It was crowded and busy. It was not a good atmosphere for Jane's creativity. But she made the most of their visit. Their rooms in 13 Queen Square were comfortable. There was much to entertain her: shopping, parties, concerts, and even fireworks in Sydney Gardens.

(left) **Jane Austen's wealthy uncle James and aunt Jane Leigh Perrot lived here at No. 1 Paragon Buildings in Bath. Note the high curb built to help keep the muddy rainwater away from the front door.** *Photo by author*

(right) **The front door of 13 Queen Square, where Jane and her family stayed in 1799 while on holiday in Bath.** *Photo by author*

After more than a month in Bath, Jane and her family returned home to Steventon Parsonage and her house in the county of Hampshire. The friendly garden, the cozy barn, and the wide-open fields welcomed them back.

Sitting frequently at her writing desk, Jane worked on her novels. She used material from Bath to develop her story *Susan* (which she would eventually rename *Northanger Abbey*). She wrote and rewrote.

On Sunday, November 9, 1800, she sat alone in the dining room. Outside, the wind howled around the parsonage . . . and then *CRASH!*

Startled, Jane jumped up from her seat.

"We have had a dreadful storm of wind in the forepart of this day," she later wrote to Cassandra, "which has done a great deal of mischief among our trees. . . . [I] went to the window, which I reached just in time to see the last of our two highly valued Elms descend into the Sweep!!!!!"

In that same newsy letter, Jane updated Cassandra with the neighborhood gossip. Their neighbor Earle Harwood injured himself with his pistol. Mr. Heathcote broke his leg in a hunting accident when his horse stepped on him. Twenty-year-old Harris Bigg-Wither "seems still in a poor way, from his bad habit of body; his hand bled again a little the other day & Dr. Littlehales has been with him lately."

Later that month, Jane went to visit Martha Lloyd, one of her closest friends. Martha's sister Mary married Jane's eldest brother, James, after his

James and Jane Leigh Perrot

Mrs. Austen had a brother named James Leigh. His name changed to Leigh Perrot when he inherited a sizeable fortune. James and his wife, Jane, were Jane Austen's wealthy aunt and uncle. They lived along the road to Bath. Uncle James and Aunt Jane also had a home at No. 1 Paragon Buildings in Bath, where Jane would visit. They had no children, so it was expected they would share some of their money with the Austens. Over the years, they did help the Austens financially from time to time. They promised to make James Austen (Jane's eldest brother) their heir.

An unusual event occurred when Aunt Jane was accused of shoplifting. Her supposed crime? Stealing a piece of lace. In Georgian England, this was punishable by exile to Australia or even death. Aunt Jane was arrested but allowed to live in squalid conditions under house arrest near the jail (spelled *gaol* in Jane's day). Whether it was attempted blackmail by the shop owners or an actual character fault of Aunt Jane's, after a difficult trial she was declared not guilty.

When one of Jane Austen's ancestors died, Uncle James and some of his cousins stood in line to inherit Stoneleigh Abbey. Jane Austen, her mother, and other relatives visited the stately mansion while the details of the will were worked out. In the end, Uncle James gave up his claim to Stoneleigh Abbey in exchange for a substantial inheritance of £24,000. He invested thousands of pounds in the bank managed by Henry Austen, Jane's favorite brother. When the bank failed, this money was lost.

Shortly thereafter, Uncle James died. His will was read. Jane Austen and her family were shocked. None of the Austens received a shilling! Instead, Uncle James left all his properties and large fortune to his wife. His will stated that at the time of Aunt Jane's death, the Austen children would inherit the small sum of £1,000 each. Elderly Aunt Jane lived nearly 20 years longer. Eventually, however, she did choose James Austen's son, James Edward Austen, as her heir.

Enjoy a Game of Whist

Card games were popular during Jane's lifetime. In her stories, she often wrote about her characters playing cards. Jane also enjoyed playing cards with her friends and family. Her aunt Jane and uncle James Leigh Perrot were fond of whist. In a letter to Cassandra, Jane wrote, "We had a very pleasant day on monday at Ashe; we sat down 14 to dinner in the study. . . . Mrs. Bramston talked a good deal of nonsense, which Mr. Bramston & Mr. Clerk seemed almost equally to enjoy. There was a whist & a casino table, & six outsiders."

Whist, a two-couple card game, was usually played quietly so players could concentrate on planning their strategies while memorizing which cards were played.

MATERIALS

- Standard 52-card deck of cards, jokers removed
- Poker chips or similar markers to keep score
- 4 players

1. The four players should pair off into partnerships, with partners sitting across from each other. Shuffle and deal all the cards clockwise around the table. Start with the player on the dealer's left and continue until all the cards are dealt. Turn the very last card face up.

2. Whichever suit is shown on this last card determines which suit (hearts, diamonds, spades, or clubs) is trump. Once everyone sees which suit is trump, the dealer adds the last card to her hand.

3. The player to the left of the dealer plays the first card. Any card may be played. Cards are always played faceup in the middle of the table. Play continues clockwise around the table until all four players have played one card, adding it to the middle. Players must play a card in the same suit that the first player in that round played. (This is usually called the suit that was *led*.) If a player does not have any cards in that suit, she may play any other card she wants to. Cards are ranked highest to lowest from Ace, King, Queen, Jack, 10, 9, 8, 7, 6, 5, 4, 3, 2.

4. One round of play (that is, when all four players have played one card) is called a *trick*. A team wins the game by taking the most tricks. How does a team win a trick? There are a few ways:

   * If no trump cards were played, the player who played the highest card in the same suit that was led wins the trick for his or her team.

* If one or more trump cards were played, the person who played the highest trump card wins the trick for her team. Trump cards are always higher than cards in other suits. (If someone played an Ace of clubs and someone else played a 2 of hearts, and hearts is trump, the 2 of hearts wins the hand so long as no higher trump cards were played.)

* If no one played a higher card in the same suit that was led, or any trump, the first player wins the trick.

5. After the first trick, the player to the left of whoever just led now leads. The lead changes each time, moving clockwise, until all 13 tricks have been played and players have no more cards.

6. Each team counts the number of tricks they took. If a team won less than six tricks, they score zero points. If they won more than six tricks, they score one point for each extra trick they took. (For example, if they won seven tricks, they score one point; if they won eight tricks, they score two points; and so on.) Each team keeps track of their score with markers known as whist counters. The team with the most points wins that game.

In Jane Austen's day, players often played a set of three games of whist. This set was called a *rubber*. The team that won two out of three games won the rubber. If you decide to play three games, instead of keeping track of all the points, you simply use the poker chips or similar items to keep track of the number of games your team won. (Whist counters were used in Georgian England and can be found online if you want to feel more authentic while you play.) The first team to collect three poker chips is the winner.

Cards dealt out for a game. *Photo by author, courtesy of the Trustees of Stoneleigh Abbey*

first wife died. Jane's visit lasted a week or more. William Austen-Leigh, along with his nephew Richard Arthur Austen-Leigh, later wrote of the trip, "When Jane returned home accompanied by Martha Lloyd, the news was abruptly announced by her mother, who thus greeted them: 'Well, girls, it is all settled; we have decided to leave Steventon in such a week, and go to Bath.'"

What? Move to Bath and leave Steventon Parsonage, their beloved home? Move away from the friends and neighbors she'd known all her life? Depart from the cradle that had nurtured her creative genius all these years?

Fye! Oh! fye!

Like the elms that crashed down during the terrible windstorm, according to the story carried down through family tradition, Jane fainted away.

Jane Austen, her sister, and her parents lived here at 4 Sydney Place from 1801 to 1804. *Photo by author*

RETIREMENT

Jane folded her best gown and packed it in her trunk along with her delicate silk stockings. She packed her papers and notebooks. She sorted through the books in her father's study and counted the shillings people paid for them at the sale. She said good-bye to her beloved pianoforte as it sold for eight guineas.

At 25 years old, Jane moved with her family to Bath. Her father had retired, and when a rector retired, he moved out of the village parsonage so the new rector could move in. The new rector was Jane's eldest brother, James, who moved back into his childhood home at Steventon with his family.

After the initial shock of relocating, Jane tried to make the best of it. Possibly she comforted herself that she could return home to visit friends and family. She looked forward to summers away from Bath to escape the intense heat. Seaside holidays especially appealed to her.

Jane, Cassandra, and their two aging parents settled into Bath. They lodged in 4 Sydney Place. Lush green trees graced Sydney Gardens, just across the street.

A PROPOSAL

Jane was never long in Bath if she could help it. After she and her parents found lodgings, they set off on a summer holiday to a cooler region.

In September 1801 she visited the neighborhood of Steventon Parsonage. She returned to Bath for the winter, but the next summer she set off again. Scholars think Jane possibly toured Wales with her family during this season. By the time autumn breezes blew in, Jane visited family and friends in her old neighborhood once again.

On Thursday, November 25, 1802, both Jane and Cassandra readied their trunks. Jane carefully packed her papers and manuscripts along with her clothes. They left Steventon Parsonage, where they had been visiting James and his second wife, Mary. They traveled to nearby Manydown, the home of the Bigg sisters and their younger brother Harris Bigg-Wither. Jane and Cassandra hoped to stay at Manydown for several weeks. At the end of December, Jane would turn 27.

One week came and went. It was Thursday, December 2. The frosty air outdoors made a roaring fire in the fireplace welcome to the sisters and friends. It had been a fine week, as visits to Manydown Park often were. There had been games and laughter and stories to share.

At one point that Thursday, Harris Bigg-Wither proposed to Jane and she accepted his offer to marry.

In the morning, however, when the Bigg sisters and Harris awoke, Jane told them she changed her mind. She made a mistake. Now her answer was no.

> "What did she say?—Just what she ought, of course. A lady always does." —Emma

There was probably distress all around. The Manydown carriage was ordered. Catherine and Alethea rode with Jane and Cassandra back to Steventon Parsonage. "A very surprised Mary received them and saw the Austens and the Biggs embrace tearfully by way of farewell."

Trunks were unloaded. The carriage clattered off back to Manydown, as Jane and Cassandra walked in with their sister-in-law.

What happened? Mary wanted to know. Why had they returned so early?

Jane gave no explanation. Distraught, she wanted to leave. She insisted that James drive them back to Bath immediately. But it was impossible, as James had to preach on Sunday. If he went to Bath, he couldn't return in time. He would be forced to ask someone else to preach.

What happened at Manydown?

Jane simply could not speak of it.

So the bewildered James agreed, at Jane's insistence, to drive his sisters back to Bath.

It remains a great mystery as to why Jane accepted Harris's proposal and then changed her mind. Many curious Janeites have conjectured all sorts of reasons, examining various clues.

Some say she first accepted the proposal because it would have meant a life of security and wealth for her and her family. As Mrs. Bigg-Wither, Jane would have been mistress of a huge estate and ruled over balls and other festivities. She could have invited her sister and parents to live with them.

Others project that marrying Harris would have given Jane a family whose members were

Harris Bigg-Wither. *Photo by author, courtesy of the Jane Austen Centre in Bath*

already her dearest friends. She might have accepted his offer at first because she cherished the idea of living at a favorite childhood retreat.

Some speculate that she changed her mind and rejected the marriage proposal because she preferred a single life. If she married, when would she find time to write? Would she be tied down with raising a family? Might she face death during childbirth as so many young women did?

Others say she wasn't interested in Harris. At 21 years old, he was nearly six years her junior. Jane once told Cassandra that Harris had bad body habits. (Nobody quite knows what she meant by that.)

If we look to her writing, we may get yet another possible answer. In her novel *Persuasion*, Anne Elliot rejects a marriage offer by her affluent neighbor Charles Musgrove. It's not because he's gruff or uncouth or unattractive. It's simply because her heart belongs to another, Captain Wentworth. Anne does not love Charles. Could it have been that Harris Bigg-Wither was not Jane's Tom Lefroy, the young Irishman who may have stolen her heart?

In her novels, Jane's heroines reject many advantageous marriage arrangements.

Why?

> "I consider everybody as having a right to marry once in their lives for love."
> —Jane Austen, in a letter to Cassandra

They want to marry for love. Was the same true for Jane?

NORTHANGER ABBEY

After Jane returned to Bath, she tried to focus on writing. Even though the visit to Manydown ended in distress, the Bigg sisters would remain her friends the rest of her life. Harris eventually married and became a respected country gentleman, the father of 10 children.

Jane pulled out her novel *Susan* (later retitled *Northanger Abbey*) and revised it again. She read *Susan* aloud to Cassandra and their parents. Her favorite brother, Henry, and his wife, Eliza, read it too. Everyone thought it was good. Very good.

Working on Jane's behalf, Henry contacted Mr. Crosby, a London publisher. It didn't take much to persuade Crosby. He thought *Susan* was good too, and he purchased it for £10 in 1803. Jane's first sale!

After this success, she picked up her pen with renewed interest and began *The Watsons*. With a busy social life and many distractions, however, work progressed slowly. In Bath, Jane could not find the time she needed to write. *The Watsons*, "a dark and unhappy novel," was never finished.

By now, all of England was as busy as the crew on Her Majesty's warship preparing for battle. After a yearlong peace agreement between England and France, the French military leader Napoleon was on the move. Jane's adventurous brother, Francis, reenlisted to active service. Her younger brother, Charles, rejoined the crew on the HMS *Endymion* as first lieutenant. On May 18, 1803,

Northanger Abbey by Jane Austen

 HEROINE

Catherine Morland

 HERO

Henry Tilney

 **HOUSE**

Northanger Abbey: Mysterious, ancient, and gothic mansion where Henry Tilney and his family live

 **OPENING LINE**

"No one who had ever seen Catherine Morland in her infancy would have supposed her born to be an heroine."

❝ FAMOUS QUOTE

"The person, be it gentleman or lady, who has not pleasure in a good novel, must be intolerably stupid."

📖 SUMMARY

Growing up in a country parsonage, one of many children, Catherine Morland has no fortune or future to speak of. When a wealthy, childless couple invite Catherine to accompany them to Bath, however, rumors circulate that Catherine will inherit riches. Old General Tilney, thinking to attach his son Henry to an heiress, permits Catherine to accompany his family home to Northanger Abbey. Caught up in the romance of reading gothic novels, Catherine Morland's imagination runs wild in her new gothic setting. Is the abbey haunted? What mysterious secrets does it hide? Thoughts of murder and foul play fill Catherine's head. In the end, upon learning the truth about Miss Morland's financial worth, the general kicks poor Catherine out of his home—but not before Henry Tilney's heart has been captured forever by her innocent and delightful charms.

(above) **Francis Austen in uniform.**
Photo by author, courtesy of the Jane Austen Centre in Bath

(right) **25 Gay Street.** *Photo by author*

war was declared between Britain and France. All along the British coast troops of volunteers marched and drilled. They wanted to protect England from a potential French invasion. Even Jane's fortunate brother Edward joined the volunteers, appointed "captain in the local battalion."

DRIFTING

Events took a sorrowful turn for Jane in 1805 when her elderly father got suddenly ill and died.

George Austen was buried at St. Swithin's in Bath, the same church he had been married in.

In the midst of their grief, what were Jane and the other Austen women to do?

Mrs. Austen had a small income. Cassandra received a small amount as well, provided by her fiancé before his death. Jane had nothing. She did not even earn money from book sales because Crosby still had not published *Susan*.

The Austen women moved to cheaper lodgings at 25 Gay Street. Jane's friend Martha Lloyd moved in with them after the death of her widowed mother, adding her small income to the household.

The Austen men tried to help. Edward promised £100 a year. James, Francis, and Henry each committed to an annual support of £50. Charles wanted to help but was in financial distress himself.

Money was tight, but Jane and the other ladies could not get jobs. Women among the landed gentry were not supposed to work. It was out of the question. Jane and the others drifted from place to place like ships lost at sea. For a while they lived with Francis and his wife at Southampton.

Word arrived one day from Edward, Jane's fortunate brother. Would the women be interested in living at the empty caretaker's cottage near the grand mansion he had inherited from the Knights? He would repair the cottage and fix it up. Jane and the others agreed. Yes!

So it was settled. In 1809 Jane, Cassandra, Mrs. Austen, and Martha Lloyd moved into Chawton Cottage.

DELIGHTFUL DAYS

Jane settled into a comfortable schedule at Chawton Cottage. Each day started with music. She "practiced daily, chiefly before breakfast."

After breakfast, Jane sat down at her writing table. She pulled out her manuscripts, the ones she had started more than 10 years earlier. She must have been delighted to be writing regularly again.

The housemaid came through the door. *Squ-ee-ee-eek*, creaked the door. Jane quickly tucked her papers away. She didn't want others peering over her shoulder, reading the thoughts she was trying to form in her unique style.

Someone offered to fix the squeak, but Jane declined. It alerted her to approaching visitors. According to William Austen-Leigh and Richard Arthur Austen-Leigh, "Her small sheets of paper could easily be put away or covered with blotting-paper, whenever the creaking swing-door (which she valued for that reason) gave notice that anyone was coming."

Jane spent the first year and a half at Chawton Cottage rewriting two of her earliest novels: *Sense and Sensibility* and *First Impressions* (renamed *Pride and Prejudice*).

Henry, proud as always of Jane's genius, made arrangements in late 1810 with the London

(left) **Chawton Cottage, Jane's home as an adult.** *Photo by author, courtesy of the Jane Austen's House Museum*

(below) **A popular fashion that young ladies such as Jane and her sister might wear.** *Courtesy of Carol Taylor, artist*

(left) Jane Austen's writing table. *Photo by Peter Smith, courtesy of the Jane Austen's House Museum*

(right) Jane visited Henry and Eliza in London here at their home on Sloane Street. *Photo by author*

publisher Thomas Egerton. Her first novel would be published anonymously so that no one would know it was written by a newcomer to the literary scene. Jane Austen's biographer Jon Spence explained, "Egerton was to bring out *Sense and Sensibility* at the author's expense." Most likely this was paid for by Henry and Eliza, since Jane had no money to speak of.

With hopes of a first novel being published, Jane waited for it to appear in print. In the meantime,

she did what every sensible writer does. She started something new.

In February 1811, she began writing *Mansfield Park*. She wrote intently, developing the characters and unraveling the twisted plot she had created.

Several months later found her in London visiting Henry and Eliza on Sloane Street. Jane had important work to do with the publisher. *Sense and Sensibility* was approaching publication. There were proofs to read, corrections to make, and edits to approve. It was an exciting time, made even more exhilarating with the round of parties, plays, and performances she attended with Henry and Eliza.

Jane returned to Chawton and to writing *Mansfield Park*. She continued to wait.

Finally, the waiting was done. In October 1811 *Sense and Sensibility* was published. At 35 years old, Jane was a published author—though the title page of the book said simply that it was written "BY A LADY."

To say it mildly, *Sense and Sensibility* was a sensation. Princess Charlotte, the daughter of the prince regent, was full of praise for it. The circle of admirers included other royalty, nobility, and gentry alike. Pray tell! who was this "lady," this clever author who had created a cast of characters so real that readers felt they knew them?

Her readers didn't have to wait long for the next novel to appear, hot off London's printing presses. *Pride and Prejudice* was published at the beginning of 1813. This time Jane didn't have to pay for it. She sold it to Edgerton for 110 pounds, a huge sum of money in Georgian England and all of it Jane's!

Fans as well as new readers grabbed every copy they could of this book whose title page stated simply, "By the Author of 'Sense and Sensibility.'" The first edition sold out, and a second edition was quickly printed. Jane felt a deep sense of satisfaction that her "own darling child" was a success.

Once again, circles of excited readers asked for the identity of the author. Neighbors, acquaintances, friends . . . all were reading Jane's novels.

Bursting with pride, Jane's favorite brother Henry could no longer keep her secret. He told anyone who praised the book that it was none other than his accomplished sister who wrote it.

Spurred on by enthusiasm, Jane continued writing *Mansfield Park*. She asked her brothers for permission to use facts and names from their naval experiences to add realistic details.

Overjoyed when she received her first published copies of *Pride and Prejudice*, on January 29, 1813, Jane wrote this letter to Cassandra saying, "I want to tell you that I have got my own darling child from London." *Courtesy of the Jane Austen's House Museum*

Pride and Prejudice by Jane Austen

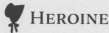 ## HEROINE

Elizabeth (Lizzy) Bennet

 ## HERO

Mr. Darcy

 ## HOUSES AND VILLAGES

Longbourn: Where the Bennets live
Meryton: Village near Longbourn where militia are quartered
Netherfield Park: Rented country home of Mr. Bingley, a young gentleman of large fortune
Pemberley: Magnificent estate of Mr. Darcy

OPENING LINE

"It is a truth universally acknowledged that a single man in possession of a good fortune, must be in want of a wife."

FAMOUS QUOTE

"To be fond of dancing was a certain step towards falling in love."

SUMMARY

Mrs. Bennet wants nothing more than to see all five of her daughters marry. But with no dowry or inheritance to speak of, who will have them? Jane, the eldest and a beauty, catches the eye of their new neighbor, Mr. Bingley. But Bingley's wealthy friend, Mr. Fitzwilliam Darcy, seems too proud to consider any prospects in the country village of Longbourn. Until that is, Elizabeth, the second Bennet daughter, steals Mr. Darcy's heart. Elizabeth will have nothing to do with Darcy, however, prejudiced against someone so proud. Then Wickham comes to town, a dashing new enlistment in the local militia. Archenemy of Mr. Darcy, Wickham is everyone's favorite, including Elizabeth's. How can she ever overcome her prejudice against Darcy and learn about his true character? And will Elizabeth ever understand her own heart?

April 1813 found her back in London at Henry and Eliza's home on Sloane Street. This visit was not to get another book published, however. Jane came to be with Eliza as she lay dying. It had been a long illness with no known details as to its cause.

After the funeral, Jane visited London again to help Henry move to Henrietta Street. It was around this time that she finished *Mansfield Park*, which was published in May 1814. Hitherto, readers had been waiting for a new title by this exciting mysterious author. Eager fans bought copies of Jane's newest novel, many declaring it their favorite. Her readers were pleased, her publisher was pleased, and she was pleased as well. *Mansfield Park* sold so many copies it gave Jane some of her best profits yet.

A Royal Admirer

In 1814, the same year *Mansfield Park* was published, Jane had already begun writing her next novel, *Emma*, a lighthearted book with a mischievous heroine. By the time *Emma* was ready for a publisher, Jane had already started writing her sixth full-length novel, *Persuasion*. Early in October 1815, she made another trip to London to visit Henry, who now lived at Hans Place.

Renowned London publisher John Murray was interested in *Emma*. What's more, Murray liked Jane's other novels and wanted permission to publish additional editions of those. Jane seemed to enjoy her negotiations with him. Murray lent Jane some of his favorite books.

> "And Mr. [Warren] Hastings! I am quite delighted with what such a man writes about [*Pride and Prejudice*]. Henry sent him the books after his return from Daylesford, but you will hear the letter too."
> —Jane Austen in a letter to Cassandra

(above) **Fanny Price, the heroine of *Mansfield Park*, receives an amber cross as a gift from her sailor brother William. This idea was no doubt based on the time when Charles Austen used prize money earned at sea to purchase these two topaz crosses for his sisters, Jane and Cassandra.** *Photo by Peter Smith, courtesy of the Jane Austen's House Museum*

(left) **The London office of the highly acclaimed publisher John Murray.** *Photo by author*

Mansfield Park by Jane Austen

HEROINE

Fanny Price

HERO

Edmund Bertram

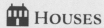

HOUSES

Mansfield Park: Magnificent estate of the Bertrams, where Fanny grows up

Mansfield Parsonage: Home of Dr. and Mrs. Grant, where Mary and Henry Crawford come to stay

OPENING LINE

"About thirty years ago Miss Maria Ward, of Huntingdon, with only seven thousand pounds, had the good luck to captivate Sir Thomas Bertram, of Mansfield Park, in the county of Northampton, and to be thereby raised to the rank of a baronet's lady, with all the comforts and consequences of an handsome house and large income."

❝ FAMOUS QUOTE

"There certainly are not so many men of large fortune in the world as there are pretty women to deserve them."

SUMMARY

As a young girl, Fanny Price is sent to be raised by her wealthy aunt and uncle, Sir Thomas and Lady Bertram of Mansfield Park. Her Aunt Norris is a tyrant. Her cousins Maria and Julia are arrogant and self-centered. Nonetheless, Fanny finds a true friend in her other cousin, Edmund. Shy, restrained, and devoutly committed to right over wrong, Fanny seems content to remain in the shadows as long as her Edmund is near. Everything changes at Mansfield Park, however, the day new neighbors move into the parsonage—brother and sister Henry and Mary Crawford. Coming from fashionable circles of London's high society, Mary and Henry operate by their own rules. Mary sweeps Edmund off his feet with her beauty and charm—yet disdains his decision to become a clergyman. Mary secretly hopes Edmund will inherit the family fortune instead. Henry, after scandalous flirtations with Maria Bertram (who was engaged to be married), targets Fanny as his prize to conquer. Will Fanny be able to withstand the pressures to marry for money when Henry Crawford proposes to her? Or will she be able to marry her true love once Edmund comes to his senses and sees Mary Crawford for who she really is?

Write a Comedy

When Jane Austen wrote Emma, *she set up her readers for a lighthearted laugh.* Emma *is a comedy of manners. It's about life, etiquette, and social blunders in Georgian England. You can use some of the same literary techniques Jane used to write your own comedy.*

CHARACTERS

Mrs. Bates is a beloved character from English literature. Why? She is not only so real but also funny. She can talk for multiple pages straight without taking a breath. And Mr. Woodhouse! He's paranoid about anything that could cause ill health. It makes for awkward situations—and good laughs.

When you write a comedy, choose comical traits for some of your characters. Here are several ideas. Give them a funny:

Physical trait, such as a dog whose ears are so long it always trips over them.

Job, such as a clown or a court jester, that can allow for silly situations.

Nickname, such as Bumble Bee McGee or Tony Baloney.

PLOT

The plot in *Emma* takes many a humorous turn. On her quest to play matchmaker, Emma makes multiple silly mistakes . . . with some of her efforts backfiring! When she tries to marry Harriet to Mr. Elton, Mr. Elton thinks it's Emma who's falling in love with him.

When you write a comedy, choose comical plot twists that will keep your readers chuckling. Here are some ideas to include:

Funny chase scene. For example, your main character's carriage could be chased by a mysterious runaway coach whose horses are out of control. Finally, the carriages stop. Your main character's love interest climbs out of the coach, seeing her at her worst—mud-splattered, shoes torn, and hair a mess.

Gossipy news scene. For example, a nosy neighbor could stop the main character in town and report that a group of monkeys escaped from the city zoo and are hiding in the main character's house. The main character rushes home, only to discover that's not true. An uncle just arrived from India with his pet monkey.

TECHNIQUES

There are other techniques you can use to write a funny story:

Silly dialogue of characters saying hilarious things.

Puns and clever wordplay, of course!

Exaggeration, such as a hat that's too big, a hundred noisy roosters, a 50-page book report due tomorrow.

Slapstick, such as slipping on a banana peel, falling into a swimming pool, bumping into a pole.

Big messes, such as honey spilled over everything, a bird that flies into the house, a bathtub that overflows.

Jane stayed in London to care for Henry after the rest of the family went home. By late October, another doctor visited Hans Place to check on the patient. Henry felt talkative.

This doctor happened to be one of the prince regent's personal physicians. Knowing this, Henry asked the doctor if he realized who Jane was.

Once again—gossipy and proud—big-brother Henry shared Jane's "secret," revealing that she was none other than the mysterious and unknown "lady" who had written *Sense and Sensibility*, *Pride and Prejudice*, and *Mansfield Park*.

Later, during a visit to the prince regent, the physician spread the juicy news. He had met an author at one of his patients' homes—but she was not just any author. She was the anonymous author to three of His Royal Highness's favorite novels!

When the doctor made another house call to Henry, the doctor told Jane "that the Prince was a great admirer of her novels: that he often read them, and had a set in each of his residences."

A new visitor arrived at Hans Place. Mr. Clarke, the librarian of Carlton House (one of the prince regent's elegant homes) was announced. He had come to persuade Jane to visit Carlton House. "The Prince," Mr. Clarke assured Jane, "had charged him to show her the Library there." He added further compliments and "civilities as to the pleasure his R.H. [Royal Highness] had received from her novels."

What was Jane to do? This was the same prince regent she had disliked so strongly when he'd rented a house near Steventon Parsonage.

Though her writing career was beginning to flourish, Jane's family suffered another crisis. During her visit to London, Henry grew deathly ill. Jane, though there to nurse him, grew alarmed. Fearful lest the worst should happen, she wrote to her family, insisting they come. James, Edward, and Cassandra rushed to Henry's side. Thankfully, Henry's symptoms grew less severe, and he was soon on the mend.

Yet, "the invitation could not be declined." About a week after the invitation, Jane dressed in her finest for her visit to the royal home.

Mr. Clarke escorted her through the rooms. He paused especially for her to enjoy the grandeur of the prince's library. It was nothing short of magnificent. Caroline Austen, Jane's niece (and biographer) said, "Speaking again of the Regent's admiration of her writing, [Mr. Clarke] declared himself charged to say, that if Miss Austen had any other novel forthcoming, she was quite at liberty to dedicate it to the Prince."

Jane "made all proper acknowledgments at the moment, but had no intention of accepting the honor offered."

When she arrived back at Hans Place and breathlessly told her story to Henry, they probably shared a good laugh. How diverting! Then Henry grew serious. In Georgian England, one didn't toy with royalty. After all, during those days a simple accusation of shoplifting could mean deportation to Australia or a death sentence. If a member of the royal family was displeased, let alone the prince regent, very unpleasant consequences could result. Jane "was advised by some of her friends that she must consider the permission as a command." As a command, it must be done. And so Jane's newest novel, *Emma*, was dedicated to the prince regent.

By December, Henry was his healthy self again. He no longer needed his sister's nursing, and so Jane "returned home, where the little adventure was talked of for a while with some interest, and afforded some amusement."

IMMORTALIZED IN WINCHESTER

Returning to her writing, Jane worked on *Persuasion*. In January 1816, with Henry's help, she bought back *Susan* from the publisher who had never published it. (During negotiations Henry did not reveal who the now-famous "anonymous" author was.) The hope was that both novels could be published soon.

The house on College Street in Winchester where Jane Austen lived her last days. *Photo by author*

Emma by Jane Austen

 **HEROINE**

Emma Woodhouse

 HERO

George Knightley

🏠 **HOUSES AND VILLAGES**

Highbury: Large and populous village where Emma Woodhouse and her neighbors live

Hartfield: Estate of the Woodhouses

Randalls: Home of Emma's former governess and her new husband, Mr. and Mrs. Weston

Donwell Abbey: Seat of Mr. Knightley

🖋 **OPENING LINE**

"Emma Woodhouse, handsome, clever, and rich, with a comfortable home and happy disposition, seemed to unite some of the best blessings of existence; and had lived nearly twenty-one years in the world with very little to distress or vex her."

❝ **FAMOUS QUOTE**

"What did she say?—Just what she ought, of course. A lady always does."

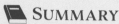 **SUMMARY**

Never planning on matrimony for herself, Emma takes up the task of matchmaking. After successfully marrying off her governess to Mr. Weston, Emma turns her energies to Mr. Elton, the new clergyman in Highbury. Emma is certain he is perfect for Harriet, her young schoolgirl friend of unknown birth. Harriet, however, has already captured the heart of a respectable farmer, Mr. Martin, so Emma must discourage that romance immediately. Matters get tangled up, especially when Emma learns Mr. Elton adores her instead of Harriet. And when Frank Churchill and Jane Fairfax arrive in Highbury, Emma's plans really get confused. Does Frank prefer Emma? Does Mr. Knightly prefer Jane? And who will claim Harriet's heart and hand? Out of the whirlwind Emma stirs up, everything finally settles just where it should, surprising Emma with a wedding of her own.

But by the time she finished writing *Persuasion* in July, Jane was not feeling well. Her back hurt. She felt tired. She was not her usual self.

Around this time several of her family members faced the threat of financial ruin. Henry declared bankruptcy. His bank had failed. Family members lost significant amounts of money. To add to these troubles, distant relatives threatened a lawsuit against Jane's fortunate brother Edward. They claimed rights to an inheritance of Chawton House and Chawton Cottage. If they won, Edward would still own his estate at Godmersham, but Jane and the Austen women would be homeless.

In the upcoming months and years, the Austen family rallied from their losses and became more financially stable. Edward was able to pay off the lawsuit by selling "most of the beech trees at Chawton Park Wood, said to be some of the finest beech trees in the land." He did not lose the house or cottage.

However, Jane was still not well. She started a novel named *Sanditon*, but it became hard to write. She was bedridden for days at a time. Cassandra stayed with her. Jane set *Sanditon* aside, unfinished.

What was the matter with her? The doctors were unsure about the cause of her illness. Her friends Elizabeth Bigg Heathcote and Alethea Bigg found a house for her in Winchester, where she could be under the care and medical advice of Mr. Lyford, a respected physician there.

She lodged at College Street with Cassandra. The Bigg sisters lived just around the corner and visited every day.

Mary Austen, the wife of Jane's eldest brother, James, came to help. Alas! it was clear the end was coming. Jane drew up her will, leaving most of her few possessions to her sister and the rest to family members and friends.

"Her sweetness of temper never failed her," remembered Caroline, daughter of Mary and James. "She was considerate and grateful to those who attended on her, and at times, when feeling rather better, her playfulness of spirit prevailed, and she amused them even in their sadness—A Brother frequently went over for a few hours, or a day or two."

On the morning of July 18, 1817, Jane Austen peacefully breathed her last.

Winchester Cathedral, Jane Austen's final resting place. *Photo by author, courtesy of the Winchester Cathedral*

Her funeral was simple, as most were in those days. The sad funeral procession left the house and walked down College Street. Cassandra stayed inside and watched from the bow window. Young James Edward Austen-Leigh was there in place of his father, James, who was ill. Brothers Edward, Henry, and Francis were also there.

The procession walked the short way to Winchester Cathedral, a stunning church Jane greatly admired. Jane's coffin was buried inside. A slab of black marble marked her final resting place beneath the floor.

(right) **Jane Austen's gravesite inside Winchester Cathedral, strewn with flowers during a special ceremony on July 18, 2017, the 200th anniversary of her death.** *Photo by author, courtesy of the Winchester Cathedral*

(below) **Cassandra Austen, Jane's sister and confidante.** *Courtesy of the Jane Austen's House Museum*

JANE AUSTEN LIVES ON

Cassandra distributed Jane's personal possessions among family members and friends. She had cut a lock of Jane's hair as a remembrance of her sister. It was probably to be set inside a glass brooch or ring. She later gave the treasure to her niece Fanny Knight to remember Aunt Jane.

Cassandra then sat down with Jane's letters. With scissors, she cut out the most personal parts of some letters and burned others. The rest she kept or gave to family members.

In 1817, the same year their sister passed away, Cassandra and Henry published Jane's novels *Northanger Abbey* and *Persuasion*.

Times were changing in Georgian England as it eventually transitioned into the Victorian Age, an era of deeper respect for religious life and more restricted morals. Henry, who had loved Jane dearly, was now a clergyman. He wrote a short biography of Jane to include with her novels. He presented to the world a quiet, religious Jane, painting her as somewhat of a recluse, a single woman who preferred to stay at home in her family circle. Though perhaps not the truest portrayal of his sister, it was a depiction he wanted her readers to believe, a portrait the world accepted until scholars looked more deeply to discover the real Jane.

Over time, sales of Jane's novels slowed and eventually died out. In 1832 Henry and Cassandra sold the copyrights for five of her books to publisher Richard Bentley. Bentley then purchased the copyright for *Pride and Prejudice* from its original

Persuasion by Jane Austen

 ## HEROINE

Anne Elliot

 ## HERO

Captain Frederick Wentworth

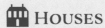 ## HOUSES

Kellynch Hall: Ancient estate of the Elliots
Uppercross Cottage: Home of Anne's sister Mary and
Charles Musgrove

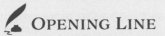 ## OPENING LINE

"Sir Walter Elliot, of Kellynch-hall, in Somersetshire, was
a man who, for his own amusement, never took up any
book but the Baronetage; there he found occupation for
an idle hour, and consolation in a distressed one . . ."

66 FAMOUS QUOTE

"You pierce my soul. I am half agony, half hope. Tell me
not that I am too late, that such precious feelings are gone
for ever. I offer myself to you again with a heart even more
your own, than when you almost broke it eight years and
a half ago."

 ## SUMMARY

Anne Elliot has lost her bloom. Eight years earlier, at the
age of nineteen, she had captured the heart of Frederick Wentworth. But Anne was the daughter of a baronet,
and Frederick was in the navy without fame, fortune, or
a title to his name. Anne's family disapproved. Her close
friend Lady Russell persuaded Anne to break the engagement. But Anne never stopped loving. Now the Elliots are in
financial distress. Forced to rent their estate, Admiral and
Mrs. Croft (sister of Frederick Wentworth) move in. Frederick is now a wealthy captain and ready to marry. Will he
fall in love with simple Louisa Musgrove? Or will Anne get
a second chance to win his heart? With a terrible accident
on the Cobb and foul play from William Walter Elliot, Esq.,
the heir presumptive of Kellynch Hall, what does the future
hold for Anne?

Self-Publish a Book

You've written a story. You'd like to get it published. Good news! There are many options in today's digital age for self-publishing your own book. If you're under 18, most will require the supervision of an adult, especially if they need to set up an account.

Explore different self-publishing options and choose the one you like best. Each publisher will offer different services.

LOCAL COPY STORE

Probably the easiest way to self-publish your book is to print it out and make copies of it at your local copy store. These typically have a variety of options for your cover and binding, such as a three-ring binder or notebook, report cover binding, or spiral binding with a cardstock cover. This is a great choice if you want to publish just one copy of your book. Jane Austen made only one final copy of all her juvenilia and printed them by hand into three separate notebooks. You can still read those today!

PHOTO BOOK COMPANY

A number of online or in-store companies now offer photo books with a variety of options and prices. This is a particularly good choice if you want to include a lot of photos in your book.

PRINT-ON-DEMAND SERVICE

The principle behind a print-on-demand (POD) service is that you don't have to buy thousands of copies of your book to pay for publication. Instead, you work with this type of self-publisher to set up a digital file for your book. When you want to buy a copy, you pay the company, and they print out a copy of your book to mail to you. This is a nice option to look into if you want to make multiple copies of your book for family and friends as well as perhaps sell your book online. Options you may want to look for as you're considering which POD service to work with include:

- A no-cost publishing track, which has a free option for publishing a book as well as options to pay for services if you want help (such as editing or cover design).
- Low cost for the authors to purchase their own copies.
- Ability to set your own sales price for the published book. This option lets you choose whether you want to set a higher price and make a profit or just sell the book at cost for others to buy at a much cheaper price. Some POD publishers set a very high sales price, and it costs a lot for you to buy your own book or sell it to others.
- Free product listing in major online bookstores.
- Option to publish as an e-book. These books are usually pretty basic with no bells or whistles, but will make your book readable on an e-reading device.
- User-friendly process with lots of online help forums. If you find a self-publishing POD service that interests you, search online for help forums to make the process easier.

DIGITAL SERVICE

Some self-publishing services go straight to e-book format without any printed book. You can publish your story as an e-book and read it on your favorite device. Some of these services are completely free to set up. You only pay to purchase the completed product. The benefit of this type of publisher is that some programs have a variety of multimedia options such as sound effects, music, or videos.

New self-publishing platforms are offered all the time. Search online and explore your options. Read customer reviews or order a self-published book to examine its quality. If in doubt, you can always try a no-cost self-publishing service and experiment with the process. Most of all, enjoy being a writer and the exciting journey of getting your book into print.

publisher. Soon after this, he published all six titles in a collection.

Bentley's publication spurred an amazing phenomenon: it began one of the greatest love stories ever to take place in the history of English literature.

Each new generation brought new readers who fell in love with Jane Austen and her books. Her novels were printed and published again and again until millions grew to cherish them and the woman who wrote them—from famous authors, such as Rudyard Kipling and Virginia Woolf, who sang her praises, to teens watching the latest movie based on her works. Today Jane Austen fans continue to grow in number and enthusiasm around the globe.

Jane Austen knew what it was to fall in love.

Jane also loved her family. She was especially close to her nieces and nephews. As her favorite niece, Fanny Knight, grew into a young woman, Jane became like a mother to her. She guided Fanny with advice about marrying for love.

Our Jane.

England's Jane.

Everyone's Jane.

Jane Austen is still guiding our hearts today.

This is her genius.

This is Jane's gift to the world.

Henry Austen, Jane's favorite brother.
Courtesy of the Jane Austen's House Museum

"Mr. Darcy sends you all the love in the world, that he can spare from me." –*Pride and Prejudice*

RESOURCES

Websites and Places to Explore

Jane Austen Society of North America (JASNA)

www.jasna.org

JASNA is the group to join if you love all things Jane—the group is involved with local book clubs to join, regional activities to enjoy, annual conferences to attend, and more. Each year JASNA also hosts a tour in England that explores various places where Jane Austen visited or lived.

Jane Austen's House Museum

www.jane-austens-house-museum.org.uk

Chawton Cottage, where Jane lived as an adult in England, is preserved as a museum. Here you'll walk back in time to touch and experience Jane's life in a personal and real way. You can also walk to church and visit the nearby "Great House" (Chawton House) just as Jane loved to do.

Jane Austen Centre in Bath

www.janeausten.co.uk

When you visit Bath in England, be sure to spend time here to dress up in costume and learn more about Jane—especially the time she spent in this city. The Regency Tea Room on the top floor is a delightful experience. And the gift shop features a fun variety of memorabilia to take home.

St. Nicholas Church, Steventon

www.stnicholascenter.org/galleries/gazetteer/1115

The church Jane attended as a child is a meaningful place to visit, with its ancient building and beautiful grounds. Many of Jane's family members are buried here. It's just a short walk to see the field where Steventon Parsonage, Jane's childhood home, once stood.

Books for Further Study

Books for Students

Ruth, Amy. *Jane Austen*. Minneapolis: Lerner, 2001.

Wagner, Heather Lehr. *Who Wrote That? Jane Austen*. Philadelphia: Chelsea House, 2004.

Books for Walking Tours

Allen, Louise. *Walking Jane Austen's London*. Long Island City, NY: Shire, 2013.

Reeve, Katharine. *Jane Austen in Bath: Walking Tours of the Writer's City*. New York: Little Bookworm, 2006.

SELECTED BIBLIOGRAPHY

Amy, Helen. *The Jane Austen Files*. Gloucestershire: Amberley, 2015.

Austen, Caroline, Henry Austen, James Austen-Leigh, and Anna Lefroy. *Talking About Jane*. Amazon Digital Services, 2012.

Austen, Jane. *Emma*. Cambridge: Cambridge University Press, 2013.

Austen, Jane. *Juvenilia: Volume the First*. University of Oxford, Bodleian Library, MS. Don. e. 7.

Austen, Jane. *Juvenilia: Volume the Second*. British Library, London.

Austen, Jane. *Juvenilia: Volume the Third*. British Library, London.

Austen, Jane. *Mansfield Park*. Cambridge: Cambridge University Press, 2005.

Austen, Jane. *Northanger Abbey*. Cambridge: Cambridge University Press, 2013.

Austen, Jane. *Persuasion*. Cambridge: Cambridge University Press, 2006.

Austen, Jane. *Pride and Prejudice*. Cambridge: Cambridge University Press, 2013.

Austen, Jane. *Sense and Sensibility*. Cambridge: Cambridge University Press, 2013.

Austen, Jane. *The Complete Works of Jane Austen: All Novels, Short Stories, Unfinished Works, Juvenilia, Letters, Poems, Prayers, Memoirs and Biographies—Fully Illustrated*. Palmera, 2012.

Austen-Leigh, James Edward. *Memoir of Jane Austen*. Transcribed by Les Bowler from the 1871 Richard Bentley and Son edition.

Austen-Leigh, Mary Augusta. *Personal Aspects of Jane Austen*. London: John Murray, 1920.

Austen-Leigh, William, and Richard Arthur Austen-Leigh. *Jane Austen: Her Life and Letters—A Family Record*. London: Smith, Elder, 1913.

Brown, Lisa. "Miss Lisa Brown's Guide to Dressing for a Regency Ball—Gentlemen's Edition." Country Dancers of Rochester website. 2008. www.cdrochester.org/flyers/MensBallClothing2008.pdf.

Chapman, R. W. *Jane Austen's Letters to Her Sister Cassandra and Others*. Oxford: Oxford University Press, 1969.

Collins, Irene. *Jane Austen: The Parson's Daughter*. London: Hambledon, 1998.

Goldsmith, Oliver. *The History of Little Goody Two-Shoes*. London: Ryle, 1847–1850. https://archive.org/details/histoflittlegood00goldiala.

Grey, J. David. *Jane Austen's Beginnings: The Juvenilia and Lady Susan*. Ann Arbor, MI: UMI Research Press, 1989.

Grey, J. David, ed. *The Jane Austen Companion*. New York: Macmillan, 1986.

Goldsmith, Oliver. *The History of England: From the Earliest Times to the Death of George II*. Vol. 4. London: 1771; University of Oxford Text Archive. http://ota.ox.ac.uk/text/5333.html.

Hill, Constance. *Jane Austen: Her Homes and Her Friends*. Bungay, Great Britain: Richard Clay & Sons, 1923.

Jenkins, Elizabeth. *Jane Austen: A Biography*. London: Victor Gollancz, 1986.

Juvenile Songs and Lessons: For Young Beginners Who Don't Know Enough to Practice. 1790–1810. https://archive.org/details/austen1671983-2001.

Knight Family. *The Knight Family Cookbook*. Hampshire, UK: Chawton House, 2014.

Le Faye, Deirdre. *A Chronology of Jane Austen and Her Family, 1600–2000.* New York: Cambridge University Press, 2013.

Le Faye, Deirdre. *Jane Austen: A Family Record.* New York: Cambridge University Press, 2004.

Le Fay, Deirdre. *Jane Austen's 'Outlandish Cousin': The Life and Letters of Eliza de Feuillide.* London: British Library, 2002.

Lefroy, Helen. *Jane Austen.* Gloucestershire: History Press, 1999.

Piggott, Patrick. *The Innocent Diversion: A Study of Music in the Life and Writings of Jane Austen.* London: Douglas Cleverdon, 1979.

Poplawski, Paul. *A Jane Austen Encyclopedia.* Westport, CT: Greenwood, 1998.

Spence, Jon. *Becoming Jane Austen.* New York: MJF Books, 2003.

"Storming of the Bastille, 14 July 1789," *World.* British Library Newspaper Archive. www.bl.uk/learning/timeline/item106472.html.

Tomalin, Clair. *Jane Austen: A Life.* New York: Vintage Books, 1997.

Tucker, George Holbert. *Jane Austen the Woman.* New York: St. Martin's, 1994.

Wilson, Kim. *Tea with Jane Austen.* London: Frances Lincoln, 2011.

Zionkowski, Linda, and Mimi Hart. "'Aunt Jane Began Her Day with Music': Austen and the Female Amateur." *Persuasions*, no. 37 (2015): 165–185.

NOTES

Chapter 1: Pride

"were usually called": J. E. Austen-Leigh, *Memoir of Jane Austen*, 2.

"We drank tea again yesterday": Jane to Cassandra Austen, from Sloane St., 18 April 1811, in Austen, *Complete Works*, loc 53905, letter 55.

"drinking tea at the Great House": Jane to Anna Austen, 10 August 1814, in Chapman, *Jane Austen's Letters*, 395.

"fashionable evening party": Wilson, *Tea with Jane Austen*, 106.

"one of the finest Estates": Jane to Francis Austen, 3 July 1813, in Chapman, *Jane Austen's Letters*, 316.

"putrid sore throat": J. E. Austen-Leigh, *Memoir of Jane Austen*, 4.

"In these situations": Austen, *Juvenilia: Volume the First*, 176.

"We are all": Mrs. Austen to William and Susannah Walter, 20 August 1775, in W. Austen-Leigh and R. A. Austen-Leigh, *Jane Austen: Her Life and Letters*, loc 571.

"Dear Sister": George Austen to William and Susannah Walter, 17 December 1775, in Austen-Leigh and Austen-Leigh, loc 581.

"cradle of genius": J. E. Austen-Leigh, *Memoir of Jane Austen*, 13.

Chapter 2: Prejudice

"Indeed no one": Mrs. Austen to William and Susannah Walter, 20 August 1775, in W. Austen-Leigh and R. A. Austen-Leigh, *Jane Austen: Her Life and Letters*, loc 577.

"Our own particular": Jane to Cassandra Austen, 21 January 1799, in Chapman, *Jane Austen's Letters*, 57.

"my poor little George": Mrs. Austen to William and Susannah Walter, 9 December 1770, in W. Austen-Leigh and R. A. Austen-Leigh, *Jane Austen: Her Life and Letters*, 548.

"bridal tour": Tomalin, *Jane Austen: A Life*, 26.

"chosen friends": W. Austen-Leigh and R. A. Austen-Leigh, *Jane Austen: Her Life and Letters*, loc 624.

"She found that only": Goldsmith, *History of Little Goody Two-Shoes*, 3.

"The Beggar's Petition": Poetry Explorer, Moss, "The Beggar's Petition."

"The beams which supported": J. E. Austen-Leigh, *Memoir of Jane Austen*, 11.

"I think, my dear": W. Austen-Leigh and R. A. Austen-Leigh, *Jane Austen: Her Life and Letters*, loc 954.

"jumping everything": W. Austen-Leigh and R. A. Austen-Leigh, loc 602.

"Mr. Austen wants": Mrs. Austen to William and Susannah Walter, 6 June 1773, in Le Faye, *Jane Austen: A Family Record*, 26.

"The wheat promises": Mrs. Austen to William and Susannah Walter, 1775, in Collins, *Jane Austen: The Parson's Daughter*, 13.

"[Aunt Jane] could throw": C. Austen, H. Austen, J. Austen-Leigh, and A. Lefroy, *Talking About Jane*, loc 449.

"Jane Austen was successful": J. E. Austen-Leigh, *Memoir of Jane Austen*, 56.

"meet the chaise": C. Austen, H. Austen, J. Austen-Leigh, and A. Lefroy, *Talking About Jane*, loc 313.

"two such hedgerows": J. E. Austen-Leigh, *Memoir of Jane Austen*, 11.

"Some of the flower seeds": Jane to Cassandra Austen, 29 May 1811, in Chapman, *Jane Austen's Letters*, 280–281.

Chapter 3: Sense

"There are no good places": Jane to Cassandra Austen, 2 March 1814, in W. Austen-Leigh and R. A. Austen-Leigh, *Jane Austen: Her Life and Letters*, loc 5021.

"stiff-mannered": J. E. Austen-Leigh, *Memoir of Jane Austen*, loc 630.

"I never, but once": Collins, *Jane Austen: The Parson's Daughter*, 33.

"of the stinking fish": Austen, *Complete Works*, loc 45902.

"were attacked": W. Austen-Leigh and R. A. Austen-Leigh, *Jane Austen: Her Life and Letters*, loc 630.

"Mrs. Cawley would": W. Austen-Leigh and R. A. Austen-Leigh, loc 630.

"Mrs. Austen and Mrs. Cooper": W. Austen-Leigh and R. A. Austen-Leigh, loc 634.

"Jane Austen was very ill": W. Austen-Leigh and R. A. Austen-Leigh, loc 634.

"If Cassandra were": J. E. Austen-Leigh, *Memoir of Jane Austen*, 9.

"she had never": Hill, *Jane Austen: Her Homes and Her Friends*, loc 379.

"both being flat": Hill, loc 379.

"The liberty which": W. Austen-Leigh and R. A. Austen-Leigh, *Jane Austen: Her Life and Letters*, loc 656.

"We are now happy": Mrs. Austen to Phylly Walter, 31 December 1786, in Le Faye, *Jane Austen: A Family Record*, 57.

Chapter 4: Sensibility

"Frederick and Elfrida": Austen, *Juvenilia: Volume the First*, iv and 1.

"The Beautifull Cassandra": Austen, 115.

"Sir William Mountague": Austen, 106–107.

"[Mr. Clifford] travelled": Austen, 112.

"The Adventures of Mr. Harley": Austen, 104–105.

"My uncle's barn": Phylly Walter to James Walter, 19 September 1787, in W. Austen-Leigh and R. A. Austen-Leigh, *Jane Austen: Her Life and Letters*, loc 1250.

"Your accomodations at": Eliza de Feuillide to Phylly Walter, 16 November 1787, in W. Austen-Leigh and R. A. Austen-Leigh, loc 1258.

"The Mystery": Austen, *Juvenilia: Volume the First*, 140–145.

"genuine warmth": J. E. Austen-Leigh, *Memoir of Jane Austen*, 33.

"clever and lively girl": J. E. Austen-Leigh, 32.

"Give us grace almighty father": Prayer reprinted by permission of St. Nicholas church in Steventon.

"sat from ten till": Phylly Walter to James Walter, 21 April 1788, in W. Austen-Leigh and R. A. Austen-Leigh, *Jane Austen: Her Life and Letters*, loc 853.

"[She] is very like": Phylly Walter to James Walter, 23 July 1788, in Le Faye, *Jane Austen's 'Outlandish Cousin,'* 86–87.

"dust & litter": Eliza de Feuillide to Phylly Walter, 22 August 1788, in Le Faye, *Jane Austen's 'Outlandish Cousin,'* 88.

"The Beautifull Cassandra": Austen, *Juvenilia: Volume the First*, 115–119.

Chapter 5: Love and Friendship

"arms against his": Eliza de Feuillide to Phylly Walter, 22 August 1788, in W. Austen-Leigh and R. A. Austen-Leigh, *Jane Austen: Her Life and Letters*, loc 868.

"The POPULAR PARTY": "Storming of the Bastille."

"The Person of the Queen": "Storming of the Bastille."

"offered to the world": W. Austen-Leigh and R. A. Austen-Leigh, *Jane Austen: Her Life and Letters*, loc 944.

"The Dutchess": Austen, *Juvenilia: Volume the First*, 92.

"300 armed Men": Austen, 94.

"The perfect form": Austen, 56.

"Reading novels": Grey, *Jane Austen's Beginnings*, 139.

"Juvenile Songs": *Juvenile Songs and Lessons: For Young Beginners Who Don't Know Enough to Practice.*

"It was the custom": Piggott, *Innocent Diversion*, 6.

"music master": Tucker, *Jane Austen the Woman*, 104.

"had a sweet voice": W. Austen-Leigh and R. A. Austen-Leigh, *Jane Austen: Her Life and Letters*, loc 4075.

"Scotch and Irish": Zionkowski and Hart, "'Aunt Jane Began Her Day with Music,'" 169.

"Tally-ho!": Tucker, *Jane Austen the Woman*, 104.

"a family whose": Goldsmith, *History of England*, loc 1572.

"A family who were": M. A. Austen-Leigh, *Personal Aspects of Jane Austen*, 27.

"Nobly said!": M. A. Austen-Leigh, 27.

"that party that": Goldsmith, *History of England*, loc 1710.

"My Dear Mr. G—": M. A. Austen-Leigh, *Personal Aspects of Jane Austen*, 28.

"disgrace to humanity": Austen, *Juvenilia: Volume the Second*, 21.

"As to the young Ladies": Eliza de Feuillide to Phylly Walter, 1 August 1791, in Le Faye, *Jane Austen's 'Outlandish Cousin,'* 103.

"I hear": Eliza de Feuillide to Phylly Walter, 14 November 1791, in Le Faye, 108.

"Cassandra & Jane": Eliza de Feuillide to Phylly Walter, 26 October 1792, in Le Faye, 116.

"We were at a Ball": Jane to Cassandra Austen, 5 September 1796, in Chapman, *Jane Austen's Letters*, 11.

Chapter 6: Persuasion

"I have made": Jane to Cassandra Austen, 1 December 1798, in Chapman, *Jane Austen's Letters*, 35.

"The general rule": "Miss Lisa Brown's Guide."

"The greenhouse": Jane to Cassandra Austen, 9 January 1796, in Chapman, *Jane Austen's Letters*, 2.

"I am almost afraid": Jane to Cassandra Austen, 9 January 1796, in Chapman, 1–2.

"I look forward": Jane to Cassandra Austen, 16 January 1796, in Chapman, 5.

"boyish love": Tomalin, *Jane Austen: A Life*, 118.

"I mean to confine": Jane to Cassandra Austen, 16 January 1796, in Chapman, 6.

"At length the day": Jane Austen to Cassandra Austen, 16 January 1796, in Chapman, 6.

"greedy detectives": Grey, *Jane Austen's Beginnings*, 174.

"I have in my": Jenkins, *Jane Austen: A Biography*, 44.

"Amongst her favorite": J. E. Austen-Leigh, *Memoir of Jane Austen*, 50.

"among them": Tomalin, *Jane Austen: A Life*, 68.

"I have made": Jane to Anna Austen, 28 September 1814, in Chapman, *Jane Austen's Letters*, 405.

"my dear Dr. Johnson": Jane to Cassandra Austen, 8 February 1807, in Chapman, 181.

"That young lady": J. E. Austen-Leigh, *Memoir of Jane Austen,* 83.

"At Devizes": Jane to Cassandra Austen, 17 May 1799, in Chapman, *Jane Austen's Letters*, 59.

"We have had a dreadful": Jane to Cassandra Austen, 8 November 1800, in Chapman, 86.

"seems still": Jane to Cassandra Austen, 8 November 1800, in Chapman, 85.

"We had a very": Jane to Cassandra Austen, 20 November 1800, in Chapman, 93.

"When Jane returned": W. Austen-Leigh and R. A. Austen-Leigh, *Jane Austen: Her Life and Letters*, loc 2732.

"A very surprised": Tomalin, *Jane Austen: A Life*, 180.

"I consider everybody": Jane to Cassandra Austen, 27 December 1808, in Chapman, *Jane Austen's Letters*, 240.

"a dark and": Spence, *Becoming Jane Austen*, 144.

"captain in the": Le Faye, *A Chronology of Jane Austen*, 291.

"practiced daily": C. Austen, H. Austen, J. Austen-Leigh, and A. Lefroy, *Talking About Jane*, loc 1631.

"Her small sheets": W. Austen-Leigh and R. A. Austen-Leigh, *Jane Austen: Her Life and Letters*, loc 4119.

"Egerton was to bring": Spence, *Becoming Jane Austen*, 178.

"own darling child": Jane to Cassandra Austen, 29 January 1813, in Chapman, *Jane Austen's Letters*, 297.

"And Mr. [Warren] Hastings!": Jane to Cassandra Austen, 15 September 1813, in Chapman, 321.

"that the Prince": C. Austen, H. Austen, J. Austen-Leigh, and A. Lefroy, *Talking About Jane*, loc 533.

"The Prince": C. Austen, H. Austen, J. Austen-Leigh, and A. Lefroy, loc 536.

"the invitation": C. Austen, H. Austen, J. Austen-Leigh, and A. Lefroy, loc 536.

"Speaking again": C. Austen, H. Austen, J. Austen-Leigh, and A. Lefroy, loc 540.

"made all proper": C. Austen, H. Austen, J. Austen-Leigh, and A. Lefroy, loc 540.

"was advised by": C. Austen, H. Austen, J. Austen-Leigh, and A. Lefroy, loc 545.

"returned home": C. Austen, H. Austen, J. Austen-Leigh, and A. Lefroy, loc 549.

"most of the beech trees": Richard Knight, great-great-great-grandson of Edward (Austen) Knight, in a speech at the Jane Austen Society of North America's 2017 Annual General Meeting.

"Her sweetness": C. Austen, H. Austen, J. Austen-Leigh, and A. Lefroy, *Talking About Jane,* loc 620.

INDEX